To Sonja Regis Vincent and Christopher.

Happy Christmas. 91

Hope you all enjoy this book.

All our Love. Paul Annette
Sandra + Nigel

The Sacred Earth

The Sacred Earth

❁

An Introduction to
The Sacred Earth Collection

by

Courtney Milne

Foreword by His Holiness
the Dalai Lama

Western Producer Prairie Books
Saskatoon, Saskatchewan

Distributed in the U.S. by
Voyageur Press, Inc., P.O. Box 338,
123 North Second Street, Stillwater,
MN, 55082, USA; (612) 430-2210/
800-888-9653

Cover photographs by Courtney Milne
Cover/interior design by John Luckhurst/GDL

Printed and bound in Hong Kong on acid free matte stock ∞
98 97 96 95 94 93 92 91 8 7 6 5 4 3 2 1

The publisher wishes to acknowledge the support received for this
publication from the Canada Council.

The author wishes to express his appreciation to Kodak Canada
Limited for its sponsorship of the Sacred Earth Project.

Western Producer Prairie Books is a unique publishing venture located
in the middle of western Canada and owned by a group of prairie
farmers who are members of the Saskatchewan Wheat Pool. From the
first book in 1954, a reprint of a serial originally carried in the weekly
newspaper *The Western Producer*, to the book before you now, the
tradition of providing enjoyable and informative reading for all
Canadians is continued.

Canadian Cataloguing in Publication Data

Milne, Courtney, 1943-
    The sacred earth

(The sacred earth collection ; v. 1)
Includes bibliographical references and index.
ISBN 0-88833-340-4

    1. Sacred space. 2. Sacred space—Pictorial works. I. Title.

BL580.M44 1991   291.3'5'0222   C91-090104-X

Contents

Acknowledgements

❋

The photographs in this book span a fifteen-year period and cover more than three hundred thousand miles (480,000 km) of travel. I wish to thank the hundreds of people who offered direction and encouragement along the way. Thank you first of all to Robert Coon, whose esoteric writings on the earth's sacred places provided the initial impetus to put the project together and helped to identify the pilgrimage which, as it turned out, I had already been on for several years. Jim Berenholtz, another modern-day mystic, also gave me a great deal of specific direction—new sites, travel tips, contacts, and helpful advice.

Shortly after my quest began, "I" became "we," when Sherrill Miller, to whom this book is dedicated, became part of my life. Sherrill superbly handled the monumental task of organizing our round-the-world trip, revealing unflinching dedication to a job that at times seemed to have no end.

Thank you to Carolynne and Mon, Kevin Dobson, and Sandi Somerville for their invaluable help providing reassurance and affirming our purpose. Thanks to Tana Dineen, Lori Labatt, Mary Ellen McQuay, Lynn Hughes, Kim Belfry, Lee Christie, Bruce Hanke, and Roy Diment for assisting us on our adventures, and to Jeff Waugh, who guided the trips to Ecuador and the Galapagos Islands. Loreen Wilsdon kept the home fires burning during our extensive travels, and Lori Sopher circulated our letters from the front lines to family and friends. Thanks to Doug Gibson for steering us to Callanish, and to Fred Mulder and his family for giving us a London base from which we launched a bevy of expeditions. Kim Gotlieb provided a home away from

home in Australia, Bill and Cecily Gregory, in Bodega Bay, California, Zulie Nakhooda in Bombay, and Bill and Lorraine Ritchie in Yugoslavia. Missi Gillespie and her Golden Bough Bookstore in Mount Shasta, California, served as an important resource. Her "purple heart" stone traveled around the world in a pouch with my camera batteries, giving me a psychic charge whenever it was needed. Terry and Tricia McFaull guided us to the hidden beauty spots of Hawaii, while Paul Lazarski and Sharron Milstein shared their special places on the west coast of Vancouver Island. Jim Allen of Ecosummer Canada showed me Ninstints and the Queen Charlotte Islands; Fraser MacLean of Great Expeditions got me first to Ecuador and later to New Zealand; Edwin Florez was my guide to the Incan sites in Peru; Hugh Culver and his colleagues at Adventure Network International landed me in Antarctica. And Rusty Reid, Doug Bell, Iona Christianson, Lee Kubica, Graham Wilson, and an intrepid Whitehorse camera club toured me around the Yukon a number of times.

My thanks to the parks personnel of Australia, New Zealand, the United States, and Canada for their kindnesses and diligent assistance, and to the many local residents who offered help around the globe. Wherever possible, we have cited these individuals and agencies by name in the companion volume, *The Pilgrim's Guide to the Sacred Earth*.

The Canadian embassies in a number of countries also went beyond the call of duty to assist us. A special thank you to our representatives in Britain, Egypt, Greece, and

Jordan, and to Robert Pounds of the Australian Embassy in Ottawa.

Thanks to Alex Tilley of Tilley Endurables, who supplied us with clothing for the trip; to Bob Gibbs of Air Canada, who helped with many little extras; and to John Melnick and his staff at Gibson Photo in Saskatoon, who cleared our shipments through customs and carefully processed 3,000 rolls of film.

Thank you to Adele Curtis, who has been of immense moral support throughout the project and who helped with the formidable task of selecting images for this book; to Nora Russell, who researched 150 sacred sites and guided the book through editing and production; to John Luckhurst for his beautiful design work; and to Elizabeth Munroe and her staff at Western Producer Prairie Books, who were willing to listen, discuss, brainstorm, and try new approaches. Thank you also to Ken Budd for his enthusiastic support and creative ideas, to Richard Popoff for ten years of color printing, and to Julian Pas, Chris Foley, and David Kelly for their expert comments and suggestions. Our appreciation to Patricia Joudry for her inspiration and spiritual guidance; and to Glen and Sherry Christianson, Gerry and Phyllis Robinson, and John Rossner, for their helpful comments as the book was taking final form.

Jack and Johnny Sutherland of TrueColor Graphics in Saskatoon gave their usual expert attention to a number of the images; Kaiu Fung designed our magnificent map of the Sacred Earth; Marlys Christianson prepared the index; and Bill Peters of Environment Canada and Breda Pavlic of Canada's UNESCO office have been extremely helpful in bringing our project to world attention.

I wish to extend a special thank you to Kodak Canada Limited for their generous sponsorship of the project.

The last bouquet is reserved for Matthew Fox whose book, *The Coming of the Cosmic Christ*, became our travel companion. His lucid descriptions of what it means to be a mystic have lent great joy and purpose to our quest for earth's sacred places.

North America

South America

CANADA
Moose Mountain Medicine Wheel 56
"Spirit Ridge" 138
"Aspen Grove" 117
Mystery Rocks 127
The Great Sand Hills 136
Minichinas Hills 149
Hudson Bay 131
Khutzeymateen Valley 132, 133
Ninstints 60, 61
Emerald Lake 85
Quetico 86
Niagara Falls 87
Prince Edward Island 118
Wikaninnish 134, 135
St. Elias Mountains 202, 203

U.S.A.
The Pacific Rim 84
Bodega Bay 82, 83
Mount Shasta 206, 207, 208, 209
Bighorn Medicine Wheel 57
Canyon de Chelly 58
Chaco Canyon 59
Cathedral Rock 204, 205
Antelope Canyon 150, 151
Mound City Group 54
Great Serpent Mound 55
The Everglades 88
Plymouth 122, 123
Rockport 126

HAWAII (U.S.A.)
Akaka Falls 105
Honaka'a 139
Lava Tree Park 140
"Paliuli" 72
Kilauea Volcano 174, 175, 176
Waikiki 71
"Kane" 173
Haena Point 106, 107
Waimea Canyon 141
Haleakala Crater 189, 190, 191
"The Rainbow" 90

MEXICO
Uxmal 35
Kohunlich 36
Palenque 37, 38, 39
Agua Azul 64, 65

BAHAMAS
Preacher's Cave 124, 125

VENEZUELA
Caruna River 104
Angel Falls 102, 103

BRAZIL
Amazon River 100

ECUADOR
Vilcabamba 154
Galapagos Islands 89
Mount Chimborazo 200, 201

PERU
Ingapirca 30
Pisac 31
Machu Picchu 32, 33
Sacsayhuaman 34
The Sacred Valley 142

BOLIVIA
Lake Titicaca 101
Copacabana 199
"Inca Creation" 214
Island of the Sun 215

Easter Island 28, 29 (Chile)

"Planet Earth" 3

CHILE
Valley of the Moon 152, 153
The Cuernos 128
"Old Man Spirit" 129

NEW ZEALAND
Cape Kidnapper's 98
Mount Tongariro 192, 193
Rotorua 148
Ruatapu Cave 146
Orakei Korako 147

Antarctica 130

Asia

Europe

BRITAIN
Stonehenge 18, 19, 20
Avebury 16, 17
The Tor 236, 237
Chalice Well 238
"Avalon" 119
Callanish 14, 15
Iona 120, 121

GREECE
The Parthenon 40
Delphi 41, 42, 43
Sounion 44, 45
Spring of Daphne 68, 69
Meteora 197

The Alps 198

Glastonbury

Athens

JORDAN
Petra 46, 47, 48, 49
Wadi Mousa 137

Jerusalem

Giza

EGYPT
The Sphinx 4
The Great Pyramid 234
The King's Chamber 235
"The Magi" 224
"The Nativity" 225
Thebes 6, 7
Temple of Hatshepsut 8
The Colossus 9
Mount Sinai 223
Chapel of the Burning Bush 222
The Nile 79, 80, 81

The Nile 79, 80, 81

ISRAEL
The Western Wall 50
Mount of Olives 227
Gethsemane 228
The Garden Tomb 229
"Earthen Cave" 230
Dead Sea 70
Spring of Pan 67
Cave of Pan 111
Sea of Galilee 226
Safed 196
Dome of the Rock 231, 232, 233
"Garden of Eden" 108, 110
Baha'i Gardens, Bahji 158, 159

Africa

TIBET
"Shambhala" 242, 243

Himalayas 194

Mount Everest 195

Ganges

Agra

NEPAL Pashupatinath
River 21.
92, 93, 94, 95

INDIA
Ellora 22, 23
Ajanta 24, 25
Taj Mahal 51
Lotus Temple 160, 161
The Bodhi Tree 217, 218
The Buddha's Cave 216
Lotus Pond 91
"Nirvana" 219
Sarnath 220, 221

CHINA
Dafu 10, 11
Wanjian Loo 116
Emeishan 168

Leshan
Chengdu

Yangzi River 73

Guilin Mountains 170, 171, 172
Reed Flute Cave 114, 115

Fujisan 162, 164, 165

Nara

JAPAN
Daibutsu 12, 13
Arike Pond 78
Byakugoji Temple 155
Daibutsu-den 12
Yoshino 156, 157
"Simono Senbon" 157
Ise Shrine 239
Jingu 240
Naiku Shrine 241
Futami Rocks 74, 75
Mount Hiei 166, 167
Shiraito Falls 76, 77

MICRONESIA
Nan Madol 52, 53

INDONESIA
Borobudur 26, 27
Dieng Plateau 112, 113
Bromo Crater 186, 187, 188
Mount Semeru 185
Gunung Batur 183
Gunung Agung 184
Air Panas 96, 97
"Golden Lotus" 62

Australia

AUSTRALIA
Lake Wabby 66
Byron Bay 99
Uluru 177, 178, 179
Kata Tjuta 180, 181
Kakadu 144
Lightning Dreaming 182
Devil's Marbles 210, 212, 213
Nourlangie 143
Fraser Island 145

The Sacred Earth

C O U R T N E Y   M I L N E ' S   J O U R N E Y

(Numbers following names refer to page numbers)

Cartography by K.I. Fung

Antarctica

Foreword

THE DALAI LAMA

This bountiful earth, like a mother, sustains us in many different ways, which is why our ancestors held her in almost religious respect. Not only does she provide the air we breathe, the water we drink, the food we eat, our clothing and shelter, but she even serves as a source of inspiration. Throughout history people all over the world have identified particular places as sacred, some because of their association with a sacred event, and others due to uplifting qualities intrinsic to the places themselves. Closely connected with this is the practice of pilgrimage.

As a deeply religious people, Tibetans have great regard for sacred places and the whole land of Tibet was protected as such. Having strong nomadic instincts, we take great joy in visiting monasteries and temples founded by great teachers, the caves of renowned meditators, sacred lakes, and mountains. Likewise, many refugees continue to make pilgrimages to the sacred sites in India, Nepal, and Bhutan. I remember being profoundly moved myself when as a young man I first visited the Buddhist holy places in India. It gave me a very special inspiration to think that at this or that place the Buddha himself had meditated and taught. Somehow I felt more closely connected to him and his teaching as a result. Similarly, when I visited Assisi I felt privileged to have joined the throngs of pilgrims who had come there over the centuries, attracted by the ideal of kindheartedness embodied by St. Francis.

This book, *The Sacred Earth*, contains photographs of sacred places in many different parts of the world. Some, like the River Ganges, are natural phenomena, some contain impressive buildings, and others are only ruins now. Taken together they represent the common need in the human quest for happiness to preserve certain places as sanctuaries, reflecting perhaps each individual's wish for inner peace. Enjoying these pictures, whether readers are reminded of their own visits to some of these sites or are inspired to seek them out, they will be able to appreciate an age-old yearning shared by all mankind.

January 26, 1991

The Quest

On a cold April evening in 1984, I curled up on the couch with a book, *Wild New Zealand*, that had just arrived in the mail. Thumbing through the colorful photographs, my hand was suddenly stilled. I was staring spellbound at an image of Red Crater, a volcanic steam vent high on the slopes of Mount Tongariro. I could not leave it alone. Something was beckoning me, indeed urging me, to climb the mountain and photograph the crater. I had no idea what would be involved in getting there, but I did know, beyond a shadow of a doubt, that I *had* to go.

Arriving in Auckland the following September, I headed immediately for Tongariro National Park, where a three-day solo trek took me up and over the saddle that lies between the peaks of Tongariro and Ruapehu. There I found Red Crater, even more glorious than the picture that had lured me to its rim. I made two hundred exposures that day, two of which appear in chapter four of this book. Though the climb through knee-deep snow was exhausting and my feet were badly blistered, I felt triumphant, but still had no idea why I had been drawn so irresistibly to the place.

On my way back to Canada, I visited friends in Hawaii, where I was told about another crater of extraordinary color and proportions named Haleakala, near the highest elevation on the island of Maui. Again, an unfamiliar inner voice demanded that I go, and the hike across the crater floor, fraught with danger and adventure, was one of the highlights of my photographic career. And once more I was rewarded with photo-

graphs reflecting the crater's austere beauty, highlighted in chapter four.

The third act of my drama took place on the doorstep of a Toronto apartment in late August of 1986. A friend had asked me what I was doing with my photography and without thinking, I heard myself saying that it wasn't the color or texture I was seeking, but rather the spirit within the landscape. As suddenly as the words were mouthed she had vanished, returning momentarily with a sheaf of esoteric manuscripts acquired under remarkable circumstances and dutifully carted home from Cuba. As I flipped through one mysterious-looking document, "Revelations from the Melchisadek Priesthood" by Robert Coon, my eye was captured by a boldly typed heading: THE TWELVE SACRED PLACES OF THE EARTH. I stood transfixed by the names on the list: Mount Tongariro, New Zealand; Haleakala Crater, Hawaii; Mount Shasta, California; Islands of the Sun and Moon, Bolivia; Palenque, Mexico; the Great Pyramid of Giza, Egypt, and the Mount of Olives, Jerusalem; Mount Kailas, Tibet; the Four Sacred Mountains of Bali; Mount Fuji, Japan; Table Mountain, South Africa; Ayers Rock, Australia; and Glastonbury, England. My heart pounding with excitement, I said, "I'm going." "Which one?" she asked. "All of them," I answered, without realizing the implications of what I had said.

Two down, ten to go, with number three right on my own continent! Two weeks later, while packing my bags for a trip to Mount Shasta, a bizarre set of circumstances began to unfold that culminated in a meeting with the woman who is now my wife. Within hours, I felt our meeting had been preordained, and together we plotted a world-wide pilgrimage in search of sacred places. We soon discovered that there were many more than twelve, as we researched and explored sites in a variety of countries. As we traveled, the list seemed to expand in geometric proportion and quickly got out of hand. By the end of a ten-month trip, it had grown to 140 sacred places, and new sites continued to emerge even as the deadline for this manuscript approached.

I should emphasize that this book represents a personal pilgrimage, and that the sites chosen are by no means all of the world's sacred places, but rather, selected highlights of what was particularly interesting to me. As a landscape photographer, I was drawn primarily to the natural rather than to the man-made sites. I was also more attracted to the older sites—places that have maintained their power for centuries, even millennia.

Although the majority of sites in this book are officially designated sacred places, there are others that do not fall into that category, but which nevertheless inspired in me a reverence and veneration often reserved for holy places alone. In these cases I am interpreting the word "sacred" in its broadest possible sense, to include awe-inspiring places where I and others have experienced a feeling of transcendence and harmony with the cosmos.

The text reflects my own personal response to the places, intertwined with facts, myths, legends, and beliefs from a variety of the world's cultures and religions. The sites are organized into chapters according to the natural features of the earth's landscape, just as these sacred locations were often chosen by aboriginal peoples for the power they felt was inherent in the geography. The sequence within each chapter is primarily governed by the flow of images themselves, although close geographical locations have been grouped together.

A highlight of my present quest occurred in May of 1990 when I spent a week on Easter Island in the South Pacific. On the second day, at a roadside stand, I saw a polished, egg-shaped rock with markings resembling our planet as seen from space. Later, its image engraved on my mind, I realized I had to have it, but although I returned several times, the stand was always closed and I eventually gave up in disappointment. Then, as I was about to go through airport security before leaving the island, a tiny woman tugged at my sleeve. "Wanna buy an egg?" she murmured. A quiet voice inside me said, listen to her. To my astonishment, she pulled the coveted stone from her satchel. I was overjoyed, feeling I had received a gift from the spirits.

A photograph of that stone is facing this page; it symbolizes for me both an overview and close-up of our sacred earth. Like a crystal ball, it offers us legacies, waters, havens, high places, and places of transformation. Let it serve as a reminder that our planet can continue to nourish us, providing gifts both physical and spiritual, if we are wise enough to heed the inner voice.

Polished volcanic rock,
Easter Island, Chile, 1990

*This book is dedicated to
my soulmate, Sherrill, a gift
from the spirit, who has brought
this pilgrim's earthly journey
a step closer to heaven*

The Sphinx

GUARDIAN OF THE TOMBS

Lying nobly by the pyramids over which he guards, and rising sixty feet (20 m) above the Giza plateau, the Sphinx has borne witness to more than forty-five hundred years of Egyptian history. His head is modeled in the likeness of the pharaoh Chephren, once entombed in the second largest of the pyramids nearby; his body is that of a lion. As part man, part beast, the Sphinx embodies both intellect and power, the perfect symbol of spiritual strength. He never sleeps but lies, motionless, watching the parade of centuries pass by beneath his enigmatic gaze, said to be invested with the wisdom of the ancient world.

In order to depict the serenity and timeless quality of the Sphinx, I photographed it at night, choosing an angle that suggested the contemplation of the universe that has fascinated mankind for countless centuries.

Sphinx and night sky,
Giza, Egypt, December 1988

Chapter One
Legacies from Antiquity

Exploring the centuries-old sacred places of our ancestors can transport us into an irresistible realm of ancient wisdom and mystery. Standing on the hallowed ground where they chose to build their monuments can help us understand how these sacred landscapes were once believed to provide a tangible link to the heavens. Hearing the wind whisper through a valley, seeing the sun rise in awesome silence, or feeling the presence of the underworld expressed in the night sky, are all experiences that can free us momentarily from our earthly ties and allow us to sense, however minutely, the eternal cosmos of which we are all a part.

But some of earth's sacred sites come to us with added gifts, presenting us not only with landscapes of great magnitude, inspiration, and power, but also with architectural evidence of how our forebears chose to express their reverence for their gods. These monuments, built in many cases thousands of years ago, can be found all over the world, sometimes in scattered remnants, other times remarkably well preserved, and almost always in overwhelming proportions and complexity, considering the technology of the day.

"Legacies from Antiquity" is by no means a catalogue of the great archaeological sites of the world, but rather a sampling of those places that were most profound for me, and that gave me, in addition, the greatest sense of identity with early peoples: Stonehenge in England, the Bighorn Medicine Wheel in the United States, the temple-fortresses of the Incas in South America, the man-made islands of Nan Madol in Micronesia, and the Temple of Karnak in Egypt, to name but a few. Visiting these sites and attempting to depict their power has affirmed for me that regardless of race, creed, language, or culture, earth's people through the ages have consistently sought to transcend their physical existence and acknowledge a spiritual power greater than themselves. And while the expressions of it may be diverse, and our individual pilgrimages quite unique, this glimpse at the works of earth's ancient builders suggests that we have been searching for common goals since the beginning of time.

Thebes

THE CITY OF CITIES

To the ancient Egyptians of what is known as the New Kingdom, Thebes was the city of cities, the beginning and the end, a dedication to the god Amun, represented by the sun. Only the remnants of the temples of Karnak and Luxor grace modern-day Luxor, signifying where Thebes once sprawled in opulent splendor along the banks of the Nile. But Amun's stature in the hearts of the people can still be sensed by the colossal proportions of the Temple of Karnak, the largest in the ancient world.

Built more than three thousand years ago, Karnak sings its proclamation to Amun with hieroglyphics inscribed on every surface of stone, lintel, pedestal, and chamber.

Particularly overwhelming is the size of the hypostyle hall, detailed opposite, a structure of 134 columns, now open to the sky. I felt like an ant, a mere speck of mortality, clinging to my tripod as I craned my neck upward trying to take it all in. The enormous chamber is like a forest of stone, the shapes of the columns inspired by the papyrus plants that grow along the Nile. A symbol of life and growth, the papyrus represents the god-force, now directly linked with the heavens because of the absence of any roof. Here, amidst this palatial grandeur, only pharaohs and priests once dared to tread.

Entrance, Temple of Karnak,
Luxor, Egypt, December 1988

Columns of Hypostyle Hall,
Temple of Karnak, Luxor, Egypt,
December 1988

Temple of Hatshepsut

"MOST SPLENDID OF ALL"

When Tuthmosis II died in 1473 BC, Queen Hatshepsut broke tradition and ruled on behalf of her dead husband, later declaring herself pharaoh, an unprecedented move. As the pharaoh was unmistakably a man in the eyes of the people, Hatshepsut took on a masculine image, even to the point of wearing the royal false beard. She ruled with an iron hand, and during her reign produced many spectacular monuments to herself. This mortuary temple cut into the rock escarpment rising from the floodplain of the Nile, built also to the glory of Amun, the sun god, is considered by many to be not only the finest in Egypt, but also one of the architectural wonders of the world. Though many of her monuments were destroyed by Hatshepsut's successors, those that remain reflect the extraordinary aesthetic sense of

Temple of Hatshepsut,
Valley of the Queens, Luxor, Egypt,
December 1988

her architects. I couldn't help noticing a marked difference between this and other Egyptian temples, in the harmony of the structure with its location. Nowhere else did I find this exquisite mirroring of the surrounding natural landforms.

The Colossus, *west bank of the Nile,*
Luxor, Egypt, December 1988

The Colossus

MUSIC OF THE DAWN

The Colossus, a huge seated statue of the Egyptian pharaoh Amenhotep III, sits with its twin on the green fields of the west flood-plain of the Nile. Towering sixty feet (20 m) high, it greets those traveling from the Nile to the valleys of the kings and queens. The two statues are all that remain of a mortuary temple erected around 1400 BC in honor of the pharaoh; the Romans later renamed them the Colossi of Memnon. Like these statues dedicated to him, Amenhotep III represented stability, ruling Egypt during a time of prosperity and peace.

What drew me to the Colossus initially, as to many of these old sites, was a wonderful story tinged with unexplained mysteries. In 27 AD the head of the Colossus fell to the ground in a violent earthquake. From that time until its restoration in the third century, the fallen head emitted music at dawn. The rich and powerful from all over the ancient world came to consult the great head, which had acquired the status of an oracle. But since its restoration, the Colossus has remained silent, neither playing its musical notes, nor whispering any clues to the mystery of their origin.

Dafu

THE GRAND BUDDHA

Chiseled from the cliff face of Linyun Hill in Leshan, Sichuan Province, China, the Grand Buddha is the largest Buddha in the world. Two hundred and thirty feet (71 m) in height, Dafu was begun in 713 AD during the Tang Dynasty by a monk named Haitong, and finished ninety years later. Haitong undertook this colossal task believing that the Buddha's presence might help to quiet the raging waters of the Min River below, which had claimed the lives of so many boatmen. The construction did subdue the river, but mainly due to the large amount of discarded granite that spilled into the holes of the river bottom.

So large is this statue that families of eight or ten can picnic on a big toe; the only way I could include the whole figure, shown opposite, was to use a fisheye lens that spanned 180 degrees.

One of the aspects that I greatly enjoyed in my study of Buddhism is its caring for the natural world. Because of its inherent harmony with nature, I found the outdoor setting to be most fitting, and I stayed for four days basking in the tranquility of the gardens. When I discovered the tree branches reaching toward the Buddha's ear, I felt as though the statue, like the religion it represents, was listening carefully to nature speaking. The secret, I thought as I lined up the right angle for the photograph, lies in developing ears large enough to hear.

Detail of head, Grand Buddha,
Leshan, China, May 1989

The Grand Buddha (opposite),
Leshan, China, May 1989

Daibutsu

TRIBUTE TO THE BUDDHA

In Nara, Japan, I found the largest bronze Buddha in the world, housed in the Daibutsu-den, the world's largest wooden building. The statue is of colossal proportions, weighing 437 tons and standing fifty-two feet (16 m) high. It was first cast in 749 AD, although fires in the Daibutsu-den have necessitated the replacement of various parts of the Great Buddha's anatomy, including the head on two occasions. The first building was completed in 752 AD, but the present structure (apart from the South Great Gate at the entrance to the temple dating from 1199) dates back to 1709, and is itself a work of art.

I had difficulty photographing the Great Buddha. No angle seemed to capture its size or dignity. I also found myself drawn into its tranquility, which left me unprepared to work with the camera beneath the overpowering influence of this image.

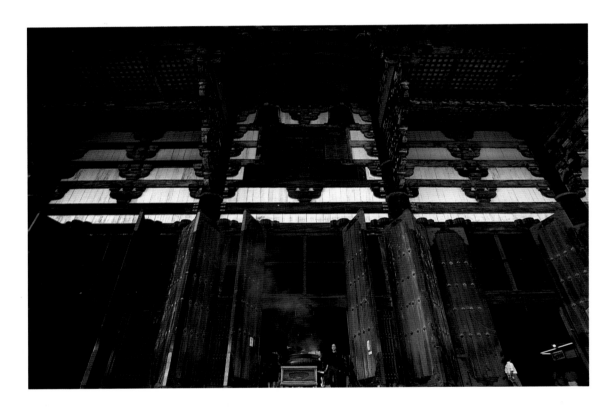

Exterior of Daibutsu-den,
Nara, Japan, April 1989

Daibutsu, Nara,
Japan, April 1989

Callanish

ALTAR OF THE MOON

Callanish, a ring of megalithic stones arranged in the shape of a Celtic cross, lies on the remote windswept island of Lewis in Scotland's Outer Hebrides. The age of the Callanish standing stones is in dispute, with the most recent estimates placing it as early as 3400 BC.

I arrived on a blustery November day, with the icy winds off Loch Roag as my only welcome. I marveled at the immensity of the center stone, rising to almost three times my height. As I gazed at it, a dark green configuration of crystals caught my eye. Was this chosen as the center stone—the altar perhaps—because of what was believed to be its magical power? One thing I did feel certain about. These prehistoric builders had positioned the stones in accordance with centuries of wisdom, leaving a five-thousand-year legacy of clues to their purpose.

Callanish standing stones at sunrise,
Callanish, Scotland, November 1988

Indeed, this ancient holy place most likely had special significance in virtually every aspect of the lives of those in the surrounding communities, serving as a meeting place, a burial mound, a place of worship, and for all the ceremonies pertaining to their physical, spiritual, and social needs and occasions. It is possible that it also served as a megalithic calendar, perhaps eight centuries earlier than Stonehenge, giving structure and meaning to the lives of those who came within its influence. The standing stones could have provided the date; measured the seasons; told the people when to plant, when to reap; and also indicated special celestial events—particularly associated with the moon—requiring acknowledgement and celebration by a people whose lives revolved around the seasons of the natural world.

During my visit to Callanish, other celestial events predominated. In one day, following a brilliant sunrise, I held my ground through snow, hail, rain, and yet more snow, the last fall adorning each megalith with a sensuous garment of white.

Callanish standing stones with snow,
Callanish, Scotland, November 1988

Standing stone and sheep,
Avebury, England, August 1989

Avebury

RING OF ENCHANTMENT

The Avebury stone circle, dating from about 2600 BC, is believed to be the largest in the world, with one hundred stones in the original construction, though only twenty-seven are still standing. The remains of many monuments and earthworks in the area suggest that Avebury was probably a significant religious center for a pre-Roman, even a pre-Druid, culture.

Unlike Callanish and Stonehenge (overleaf), Avebury has no obvious astronomical alignments. Fragmentary evidence on the site suggests ceremonies pertaining to fertility rites. And whereas both Callanish and Stonehenge are compact, massive stone circles dominating the surrounding landscape, the stones at Avebury, though enormous, are unobtrusive in their placement, meandering through the contemporary village town. It is not unlike a scavenger hunt to follow the thread of stones across streets, back and forth over the main highway, around houses, and across pastures of sheep and cattle.

Avebury belongs to the morning, to the soft dampness of dew-kissed grasses and the misty mauves of a predawn dreamscape. The only sounds mingling with the silence are the occasional tinny clack of a sheep bell or the continuous brushing and chewing of a calf clearing the base of the stones of excess grass. I could easily have stayed a month in this utopia, rising early, strolling among the stones, talking to the animals, and letting the rest of the world carry on at its frenzied pace.

Dawn mist, *Avebury,*
England, August 1989

Stonehenge

MEGALITHS OF MYSTERY

Shrouded in the mist of its prehistoric past, Stonehenge thrusts upward in the middle of Salisbury Plain in southern England. Awkwardly distorting the rounded hillside, the ruin appears almost apologetic for its intrusion in the modern world. Yet despite its ungainly, lop-sided, and somewhat dilapidated appearance, this ancient double ring of megaliths has a dignity that invites reverence.

Built in several stages beginning around 3100 BC, Stonehenge was mysteriously abandoned some centuries before the birth of Christ, and although it is the best known of Britain's nine hundred stone circles, astonishingly little is understood about the origin and purpose of the stones. It is clear the whole area was regarded as sacred ground because of the large number of burial mounds in the vicinity. But I smile each time another scientist speculates. For me, the power of Stonehenge lies in its mystery; the stones themselves are guardians of the

Stonehenge standing stones with flashlight and moon, Amesbury, England, August 1989

secrets. Some scholars have shown that Stonehenge may have been a highly sophisticated observatory. Alignments of the stones correspond with the paths of the sun, moon, and stars during certain significant celestial occurrences, providing a sophisticated calendar of seasonal events.

Stonehenge at dawn with moon,
Amesbury, England, August 1989

One morning shortly after sunrise, I watched the mists envelop Stonehenge in an ethereal light. For an instant the megaliths seemed to shed their earthly weight and float like spirits in an enchanted realm.

Stonehenge with mist at sunrise,
Amesbury, England, August 1989

Pashupatinath

TEMPLE OF SHIVA

Away from Katmandu's city center, on the banks of the sacred Bagmati River, stands one of the holiest temples of the Hindu world. Pashupatinath is dedicated to Lord Shiva, one of the supreme Hindu deities. In February of each year thousands of Hindus make pilgrimage to Nepal from all parts of India to take part in rituals that include bathing, singing, and fasting. Though only Hindus are allowed into the inner courtyard of the temple, anyone is welcome to the temple grounds. The day I visited Pashupatinath there were few pilgrims. The long set of stone steps leading from the river up to the temple was strangely quiet, as if preparing for the next great wave of humanity. The few Hindu women who did make the steep climb provided a striking accent in their colorful saris, warmed by the rays of the late afternoon sun.

Woman and steps, Pashupatinath Temple,
Katmandu, Nepal, March 1989

Ellora

TEMPLE OF KAILASA

In India, one learns to meditate despite the superfluity of external noise and adverse conditions. Sacred places are within one's heart. This attitude must have prevailed for the craftsmen at Ellora, a row of caves and temples carved out of the rock escarpment near Aurangabad over twelve hundred years ago. The exquisite beauty of the carvings is inspired work, particularly the Temple of Kailasa, probably the single greatest piece of artwork in India, and without question, its finest stone sculpture. According to local legend, even the master-builder, Visva-Karma, stood back from his finished temple and said, "I could not have built this; it is too magnificent."

The Kailasa Temple is the symbolic abode of Lord Shiva and a multitude of other Hindu gods in various manifestations—an encyclopedia of Hindu mythology in rock, rivaling the Javanese stupa of Borobudur, visited later in this chapter. The main temple complex, with its steep sides representative of the holy Mount Kailas, is surrounded by other multileveled temples, galleries, pavilions, porticos, porches, and courtyards; every angle is filled with life-sized human and animal figures from the Hindu holy books. Symbolizing its colossal size, the Kailasa Temple is flanked by a row of elephants lined up at its base as though they are supporting the entire weight of the building on their backs.

Kailasa Temple, *cave #16 at Ellora, India, February 1989*

Detail of elephants, *Kailasa Temple,*
cave #16 at Ellora, India,
February 1989

Ajanta

SYMPHONY OF STONE

The sculptures and paintings of the Ajanta caves are in many respects the Buddhist counterpart of Ellora; they are thought by many to be the greatest collection of cave artwork in India. The thirty excavations, in the former native state of Hyderabad, were constructed from the second century BC to about the seventh century AD, a period during which the Deccan region of western

Interior of cave #16,
Ajanta, India, February 1989

India experienced the Golden Age of Indian art. The landscape, with its dramatic out-croppings, spectacular valleys, and accessible cliffs, made Ajanta a utopia for Buddhist monks seeking nirvana, their state of perfect bliss, and for artisans seeking an idyllic spot to perform their miracles in stone. One witness to the caves' interiors called Ajanta "a rare symphony of three arts—architecture, sculpture, and painting."

Although the cave paintings at Ajanta are world famous, I was drawn more to the stone sculptures. My favorite, the reclining Buddha, on the verge of attaining nirvana, stretched the entire length of one cave wall.

Below him are his disciples, distraught at the thought of his leaving them, while above him the heavenly spirits rejoice and prepare for his arrival. I used a long shutter speed to photograph the Buddhist pilgrims filing by in their white tunics. For me, they too represent spirits in search of their nirvana, sharing this heavenly moment with the Buddha.

Reclining Buddha, cave #26, Ajanta, India, February 1989

Borobudur

STAIRWAY TO NIRVANA

Borobudur, the biggest stone structure in the southern hemisphere, and the largest Buddhist stupa in the world, is located in central Java, a part of Indonesia. Built in the ninth century AD over a pre-existing earth mound, it was constructed as a monument to Mahayana Buddhism, which asserts that one's good conduct on earth can release the soul from its state of suffering. Though the mass of Borobudur is gigantic, the overall impression is of a rather low, flat building. Its shape is said to have been determined by the Buddha folding his beggar's cloth to form the square base, inverting his beggar's bowl to make the hemispheric middle, and adding his walking stick for the pinnacle. Buddhist belief encompasses three spheres of existence, which are symbolically represented in the monument. The square base is for sinners. Immediately above that, the five ascending terraces of diminishing size represent the search for salvation. And finally, the three uppermost terraces portray nirvana, the ultimate sphere of timeless bliss.

Detail of upper terrace,
Borobudur, Java, June 1989

It was difficult for me to experience bliss at Borobudur when each visit was met with torrential downpours, but my Javanese guide dutifully held the umbrella while I traced the sequence of the Buddha's life on the twenty-seven hundred carved panels. My most enlightened moment arrived with a lull in the rains, allowing a brief glimpse at the majesty of the surrounding jungle.

View from upper terrace,
Borobudur, Java, June 1989

Easter Island

LAND OF ANCIENT STATUES

Easter Island is said to be the loneliest island on earth because it is so far from any other land. Situated in the middle of the South Pacific, it is equidistant from Tahiti to the west and South America to the east. The island is best known for its giant stone carvings, only a small number of which are presently standing; hundreds lie face down where they have toppled, or face up in their original quarry, from which they have never been set free. One unfinished torso measures over sixty-five feet (20 m) long and weighs three hundred tons. Though a number of theories have been advanced, it is a great mystery how these colossal statues, dating as far back as 400 AD, were moved.

What is better understood is the origin of their builders. Present language patterns and skeletal remains indicate that they came from Polynesia. It is believed that the sculptures represent ancestors, many of whom became rulers of Easter Island; their statues were placed as guardian spirits in surrounding villages. Eventually, tribal wars ensued, and the statues, revered as sacred symbols, were knocked down. Thirty of the original eight hundred have been resurrected during this century.

I remained on the island for a week, making day-long trips across its twenty-mile (32 km) width. Though my photography kept me busy, I felt that time had ceased and that a spell had been cast over me by the aura of these spirits and the caress of the south sea wind.

Stone carvings at Rano Raraku,
Easter Island, Chile, May 1990

Sunset light, Rano Raraku,
Easter Island, Chile, May 1990

Ingapirca

LAST STRONGHOLD OF THE INCAS

Ingapirca, a giant fortress propped on the slopes of the Andes fifty-five miles (88 km) from Cuenca, is Ecuador's only accessible remnant of the Inca Empire, which once dominated an enormous area along the west coast of South America. Built near the end of the fifteenth century by Huayna Capac, the last Inca leader, it was one of the final great strongholds to be constructed before the Spanish invasion in 1532. At first glance it might appear that Ingapirca is just another fortress, but closer examination reveals carefully engraved rock, meticulous measurements, and perfectly positioned alignments, suggesting an additional role as an observatory or temple complex for religious ceremonies.

As I approached the main portal to the inner courtyard, a young peasant girl sat regally on the top step, framing herself in the trapezoidal doorway, one of the hallmarks of Incan construction. She covered her mouth with her small woven blanket, partly, I suspect, because of the cold and partly due to shyness, although her eyes shone proudly and without fear.

Ingapirca has two stone faces that seem to guard the fortress. They were called Intinahui, meaning "eyes of the road." But for me the true guardians of Ingapirca are the two brown eyes of this nameless child, bringing warmth and dignity to these tired old stones.

Girl on step, Royal Palace,
Ingapirca, Ecuador, February 1986

Pisac

FORTRESS CITY OF THE INCAS

Perched like a condor's nest high above the Sacred Valley in Peru, Pisac is a ruin of the largest fortress city of the Incas. Built probably in the midfifteenth century, it commands an inspiring view across an enormous ravine, gazing almost straight down to the Quitamayo River. Mysteriously, Pisac was never mentioned in Incan history, despite its size, its magnificent masonry, and the fact that its natural defenses and terraced constructions were virtually impenetrable.

Like Machu Picchu (overleaf), Pisac was richly endowed with temples and shrines to commemorate the Inca sun god. As in many ancient cultures, the Incas saw little distinction between astronomy and religion. To understand the movements of the sun, moon, and stars was to be in touch with the great beyond. Still visible at Pisac is the sun dial, a sacred rock that stood at the center of Intihuatana, the "hitching post of the sun." The Incas believed that if they symbolically tied the sun to these ritually sculpted rocks, they could prevent it from disappearing completely during the winter solstice. Perhaps they were right. During my visit to Pisac, the rope was gone from the rock and it rained intermittently throughout the day.

Ruins at Pisac,
Peru, January 1988

Machu Picchu

SACRED CITY OF THE ANDES

South America's most famous ruins, the remains of Machu Picchu, are tucked into the saddle between two mountain peaks deep in the heart of the Peruvian Andes. From the Urubamba River twenty-three hundred feet (700 m) below, there is no sign that Machu Picchu even exists, and I wondered if I had left the train at the wrong stop as I peered up, trying to catch some glimpse of the celebrated Incan hideaway. Even upon arrival at the site there was no sign of civilization until I rounded a bend on a narrow footpath, and suddenly it all lay before me. Here were walled terraces, temples, roofless stone houses, huge ceremonial rocks, courtyards, streets, stairways, and plazas, all laid out in perfect harmony with the contours of the land and all with commanding views, yet hidden from would-be marauders.

Though the Incas did not build Machu Picchu until the fifteenth century, it was never discovered by the Spanish armies, and it flourished, probably as a sacred fortress for nobility, long after the Spanish dominated Peru.

View from Funerary Hut,
Machu Picchu, Peru, January 1988

Because of the high proportion of female skeletons found at the site, some believe that Machu Picchu may have been a religious sanctuary presided over by the Inca's chosen women. Whether that is true or not, it was certainly a place of worship, so carefully constructed that one cannot deny the significance and stature it must have had for its makers.

The setting took my breath away, and as I climbed high above the main city to the Funerary Rock and the House of the Caretaker, I felt that the Incas had revealed to us how, in one motion, we could reach for the heavens and also live in harmony with the earth.

Detail of wall, fig tree in window,
Machu Picchu, Peru, January 1988

Sacsayhuaman

TRIBUTE TO THE GODS

As I stood on the knoll above Sacsayhuaman, the temple fortress overlooking the ancient Incan capital of Cuzco in Peru, I was captivated by the mystery of the place. The hundreds of stones comprising the terraced fortifications are massive, the masonry a study in perfection. It was almost inconceivable that each stone of these ramparts, with weights up to 126 tons, had been painstakingly carved and moved into place by human hands. Certainly the workmanship was brilliant, but it was more than that—it was inspired. Beginning sometime after 1445, twenty thousand laborers with primitive tools worked on these stones with a patience and reverence that we in the twentieth century cannot fully appreciate.

My Peruvian odyssey led me to Edwin Florez, a man living in Cuzco, who was well-versed in Incan history. Escorting me to Sacsayhuaman, he explained that although this site is popularly known as a fortress, it was equally important to the Incas as a shrine, a temple to the sun, its mighty ramparts enclosing scenes of elaborate ceremony and worship as well as military activities.

Detail of fortress, *Sacsayhuaman, Peru, January 1988*

Uxmal

TEMPLE OF THE MAGICIAN

The sheer size of the buildings and the copious ornamentation at Uxmal in Mexico's Yucatan Peninsula mark it as a center of great importance. Indeed, it was not only the legendary home of a magician-king, but also the northern capital of the Maya, a culture that flourished in Central and South America from the fourth to the tenth century AD. Uxmal boasts the finest craftsmanship and opulence in pyramids, palaces, and terraces, many of which are without rival in the Mayan civilization.

Among these, the Temple of the Magician stands out as a spark for the imagination. This elaborately ornamented temple, perched at the apex of an enormous oval pyramid and built around 569 AD, is the focus of a Mayan tale associated with one of their benevolent rulers, a dwarf with extraordinary powers who is reputed to have hatched out of an egg. A series of events molded by prophecy, magic, trickery, and wit combine to help him pass the apparently insurmountable tests that will make him ruler of Uxmal. Supplanting a wicked king, he ruled with wisdom and compassion from the edifice built in his honor, the Temple of the Magician. I juxtaposed the temple and a branch of bougainvillea, its brilliant color emblematic, for me, of the dwarf's indefatigable vitality.

Temple of Magician and bougainvillea,
Uxmal, Mexico, March 1988

Kohunlich

PYRAMID TEMPLE
OF THE MASKS

Still largely hidden amidst the jungle at the base of Mexico's Yucatan Peninsula, this Mayan city, remnant of a culture that flourished a thousand years ago, has only five of its estimated two hundred buildings excavated. Kohunlich is off the beaten path and has few visitors, yet it stands unique, boasting six huge stone masks that line the steep, broad stairway to the Temple of the Sun. This is the domain of Kinich Ahau, the sun god, whose spirit dwells in the masks themselves, and whose eyes defy one to ignore his presence. Though the mask shown here was off to the side of the great stairway, it drew me to stand before it, and I felt mesmerized by the intensity of its stony gaze.

Stone mask, Kohunlich ruins,
Mexico, February 1988

Palenque

TEMPLE CITY
OF THE MAYA

Well over a thousand years ago, Mayan royalty commissioned the building of a temple city in honor of their sun god. This was Palenque, which became a ceremonial center that quickly dominated the area; it also represents the height of artistic achievement in Mayan architecture. Today, its remains nestled in the jungles just south of Mexico's Yucatan Peninsula, it retains all the charm and dignity it must have held at the zenith of its power. Much of Palenque has been restored, but the aura of antiquity surrounding the ruins made me feel as if I were walking into a romantic fairy tale, although it must be acknowledged that Mayan society was far from ideal.

Royal Palace, *Palenque, Mexico, March 1988*

I was drawn to the Temple of Inscriptions, one of the holiest places at Palenque. In the glow of the morning light, the long stairway, climbing steeply from the central courtyard, seemed like steps to heaven. The temple was in fact built to house the funerary crypt of a seventh-century ruler, Lord Pacal, although its use as a tomb was not discovered until 1952.

Temple of Inscriptions,
Palenque, Mexico, March 1988

One morning as I walked through the vaulted arches of the outer palace at Palenque, the first rays of sun beamed through the hallway, landing on a stone slab. Before my eyes, the rock turned to gold, testimony that the sun god still reigns supreme at Palenque, performing his magic at the dawn of each new day.

Morning light in hallway, *Royal Palace, Palenque, Mexico, March 1988*

The Parthenon

TEMPLE TO ATHENA

Built about 440 BC in honor of Athena, goddess of war and personification of wisdom, the Parthenon as it stands today is the fourth in a series of temples to have been built on the site since the seventh century BC. It stands on an elevated rock promontory known as the acropolis in the center of Athens, Greece, where the goddess who gave her name to the city has been worshipped since the sixteenth century BC. The Parthenon is regarded by many as the world's most magnificent monument; its classically perfect proportions have been an inspiration to artists and architects throughout its long history and have served as a standard for many other temples and buildings.

While I marveled at the elegance and grandeur of the structure, I also felt a sadness for its sorry state of repair. This temple, which has withstood the desecration of barbarians and more modern warfare, earthquakes and other ravages of time, and "benevolent" dismantling by antiquarians eager for museum artifacts, now faces by far her greatest enemy—pollution. Restoration work began on the Parthenon over 150 years ago and continues to the present day. The corner shown in this photograph was, at the time of my visit, the only portion of the building unencumbered by scaffolding.

Detail of the Parthenon on the Acropolis,
Athens, Greece, January 1989

Delphi

HOME OF THE EARTH GODDESS

Delphi, home of the most famous oracle of the
ancient world, is a cluster of temples, shrines, a
stadium, and a sports field tucked into the
hillside on the south slope of Mount Parnassus
in Greece. Built about 1000 BC, Delphi reached
the height of its fame around two hundred years
later, and flourished for some time before being
sporadically plundered and eventually closed by
the Christians in the fourth century AD.

*__Stone seating, Sports Field__,
Delphi, Greece, January 1989*

According to the ancient Greeks, Delphi was believed to be the center point of the earth, symbolized by a huge ornately carved rock called the omphalos, meaning "navel," and home to Phytho, the earth goddess. Legend has it that Apollo, the sun god, slew the serpent that protected Pytho's oracle and set up his own, employing priestesses called pythias to provide prophecies for clientele from all over the ancient world. The oracle was justly famous for the ambiguity of its pronouncements. A classic account was that of Lydia's King Croesus, who asked if he should attack the Persians, and was told that he would destroy a great empire if he did so. Ironically, the empire he destroyed was his own.

The pythias sat on three-legged stools called tripods placed over vents where intoxicating vapors emanated from the earth, inspiring their utterances. I carried my tripod down the hill to the Temple of Athena, which coincidentally now stands with only three columns intact. Here, on a warm clear night with a full moon smiling overhead, there is little problem communicating directly with the earth mother, and giving Apollo and his pythias the night off.

Temple of Athena, Delphi, Greece, January 1989

Temple of Athena and moon,
Delphi, Greece, January 1989

Sounion

HEADLAND OF POSEIDON

At the crest of a rocky promontory rising from the Bay of Sounion in Greece stands a temple of exquisite proportions. Dating from 444 BC, the Temple of Poseidon has thirty-four splendid Doric columns of grey-veined marble, and from the Ionian Sea almost two hundred feet (60 m) below the temple base, seafarers through the ages have marveled at its pristine beauty. From the sea, the columns glow dazzlingly white against the royal blue skies of southern Greece. Like its patron, Poseidon, Greek god of the sea, the temple dominates the waters, casting a spell over fishermen and land-dwellers alike.

Although exposed to the furious westerlies of Cape Sounion, Poseidon's temple also once provided a haven for those seeking refuge. As I gazed down at the sea disappearing into the evening mists, I wondered how many seamen's lives had been spared because they were able to pinpoint Poseidon's white temple, like a beacon in a storm.

Temple of Poseidon, *Sounion, Greece, January 1989*

Temple of Poseidon and setting sun,
Sounion, Greece, January 1989

Petra

ROCK CITY OF
THE NABATEANS

Petra is a city carved out of glowing sand-stone cliffs that rise dramatically out of the Jordanian Desert northeast of the Gulf of Aqaba. Dating to 400 BC, Petra was once the ancient capital of the Nabateans, originally a nomadic Arab tribe. The entrance to this enclosed city is through the Siq, a narrow cleft in a spectacular rock face, in some places barely wider than the axle of a pair of chariot wheels.

I followed the Siq on foot for about a mile (1.5 km), stopping every moment or two for the dust to clear and then capturing yet another exposure of the red sandstone walls catching the morning glow and bouncing the sunlight down the canyon walls in a cascade of ochres, blues, purples, and pinks. Little did I realize that this symphony of light was but a muted prelude to the grand march: the sacred city of Petra.

The Pharaoh's Treasury from the Siq,
Petra, Jordan, December 1988

Rounding the last bend, the Siq opens onto a courtyard dominated by the magnificent sun-drenched facade of Khasneh al Faroun, the Pharaoh's Treasury. The first glimpse, through an uneven vertical window, left me wondering if I had walked into a dream world. Like all the architecture at Petra, the Treasury is entirely sculpted from the living rock. With its elegantly carved exterior, its classical beauty, exquisite proportions, and its almost flawless condition, the Treasury has been an inspiration to travelers since its "discovery" by westerners in the early nineteenth century.

Accessible even today only on horseback or on foot (with the occasional horse-drawn buggy from the tourist hotel), Petra must have seemed to ancient visitors a place unto itself. Yet it lay at the crossroads of two important trade routes of the ancient world. At the height of its glory, before the seventh century AD, it housed twenty thousand people, but now all the standing structures have vanished; only the tombs, temples, shrines, and cloistered rooms remain, carved out of the rose-colored shoulder of an almost inaccessible range of cliffs.

The Pharaoh's Treasury,
Petra, Jordan, December 1988

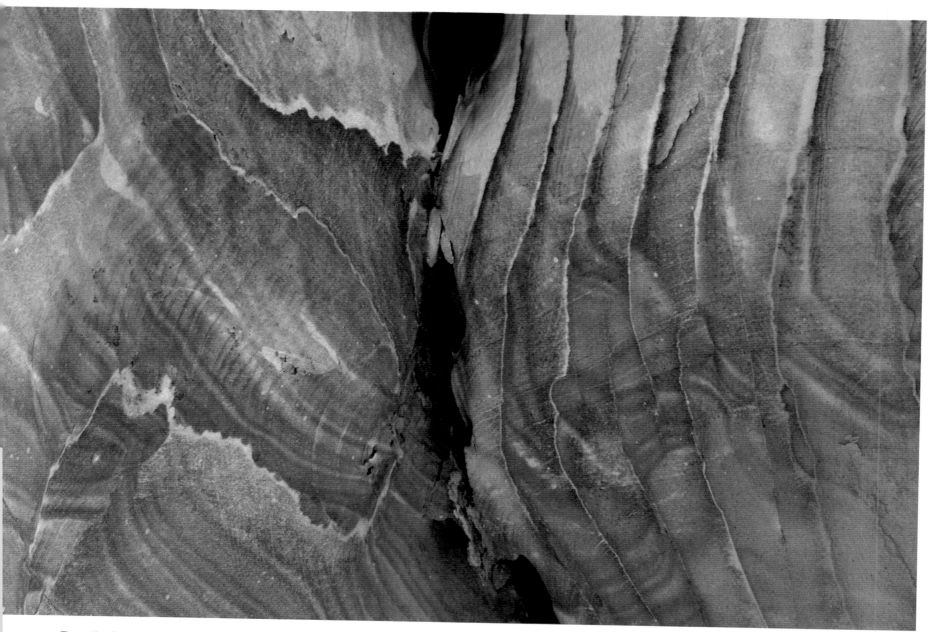

Detail of sandstone wall,
Petra, Jordan, December 1988

Exterior of cave wall,
Petra, Jordan, December 1988

The Western Wall

PLACE OF THE
DIVINE PRESENCE

The Western Wall, often referred to by outsiders as the Wailing Wall, is thought to be a remnant of the outer court of Herod's magnificent temple, built sometime after

Solomon's original temple on the site was destroyed in the sixth century BC. Herod's temple was virtually razed by the Romans in 70 AD, and thereafter, there was a Roman temple on the site until the empire was Christianized. The site was abandoned for some considerable time, until Moslem architects in the seventh century cleared the debris to build the early mosque complex.

Tradition has it that the "Divine Presence" remained among the ruins of Solomon's temple for a period following its destruction, and then departed. The wall as it stands today is sacred because of its associa-

Western Wall, Jerusalem, Israel, December 1988

tion with the temple where God dwelt among his people; it came to symbolize the longing of the Jews for a gathering from exile and a return to the Holy Land. It remains a link between an oppressed people and their God, an assurance that their prayers will be heard. I was moved by the serenity of those standing at the wall, and though cameras are not forbidden, I felt led to make my exposures from a discreet distance.

Taj Mahal

MONUMENT OF LOVE

Shah Jehan, the fifth Moghul emperor of India, had the Taj Mahal built during the early years of the seventeenth century in memory of his wife, Mumtaz Mahal, who died giving birth to their fourteenth child. As the favorite of four wives, not to mention the five hundred ladies of his harem, she was legendary in her loyalty, love, and support of his rulership. He held her in equal affection and esteem, and withdrew into two years of mourning after her death. Twenty thousand workers labored for twenty-two years to create the world's most famous mausoleum, fulfilling Mumtaz's deathbed wish that a monument of perfect proportions and beauty be built to symbolize their love.

When I first entered the opulent gardens at Agra, I was amazed that the Taj Mahal could accommodate so many guests without seeming to be overwhelmingly crowded. In

Procession in courtyard,
Taj Mahal, Agra, India, March 1989

spite of the hundred thousand souls who make pilgrimage here every day, a peacefulness permeates the landscape of carefully manicured lawns, sculpted trees, and brightly flowered courtyards. The Taj Mahal is a haven large enough to receive all faiths and all walks of life, endowing even the poorest pilgrim with a richness of spirit.

Nan Madol

REEF OF HEAVEN

The ruins of Nan Madol lie off the east coast of the island of Pohnpei (Ponape) in Micronesia, formerly known as the Eastern Carolines. Here, in a primitive setting of tropical vegetation, ninety-two man-made islets rise from the shallow waters of the Pacific, twenty-seven hundred miles (4,320 km) southwest of Hawaii. Like present-day Venice, the islets of Nan Madol are linked by a network of canals, easily navigable by canoe at high tide, but only ankle deep at low tide.

Originally called Soun Nal-leng (Reef of Heaven), this ancient royal city held me in its grip as tightly as the hibiscus and mangrove clutched at the basalt boulders that had long since lost their fight to maintain a secure position on the walls. The earliest construction dates from 500 AD, when Nan Madol became the headquarters for a powerful local tribe known as the Deleur, who built their fortifications, palaces, temples, and terraces from basalt columns and boulders floated from quarries on the mainland. The Deleur ruled Pohnpei until the early 1600s, when disease from outside sources eradicated their empire. Nan Dauwas, their royal mortuary compound, is the crowning showpiece of Nan Madol, with walls rising at the corners to almost four times my height. Despite their dilapidated state, the walls felt strangely protective, as though they would help me if I would take the time to unravel their mysteries.

Ruins at Nan Dauwas, *Nan Madol, Pohnpei, Micronesia, June 1989*

Nan Dauwas and predawn sky,
Nan Madol, Pohnpei, Micronesia, June 1989

Hopewell Burial Mounds

CITY OF THE DEAD

Three miles north of present-day Chillicothe, Ohio, lies one of North America's most ancient legacies, the Mound City Group National Monument—twenty-three burial mounds surrounded by a low earthen embankment. Sycamores, maples, and cottonwoods adorn this "city of the dead," which is believed to date back to 200 BC, and is attributed to the Hopewell Indian culture of mound builders. The Mound City group appears to be the center of a culture that extended along the western edge of the Appalachians for about a thousand miles. These mounds must have housed the most honored of the population, judging from the magnificent artifacts found among the graves.

I visited the area in late October during nature's final triumphant blaze of glory. As I watched the leaves fluttering to the ground, shrouding the grassy mounds, I wondered if the Hopewell people's belief in an afterlife could have been encouraged by observing the seasonal cycles of nature, by the knowledge that after winter's "deaths" inevitably comes a season of rebirth and new life.

Grass-covered burial mound,
Mound City Group National Monument,
Chillicothe, Ohio, October 1990

The Great Serpent Mound

SYMBOL OF MYSTICAL POWER

The Great Serpent Mound, the largest and best known of America's so-called effigy mounds, winds across a forested hilltop near the town of Peebles in Adams County, Ohio. This giant earthen snake, constructed over two thousand years ago, is about twenty feet wide, four feet high, and if extended to its full length, would measure 1,348 feet long (6 m x 1.2 m x 415 m). Its seventeen-foot (5m) jaws are stretched around an oval-shaped egg, which it appears about to swallow. Although there is some disagreement as to whether it was built by the Hopewell or the Adena Indian culture, whatever its purpose, it was not a burial mound, as no human remains have been unearthed.

For me, the huge snake gains its strength

Aerial view of the Great Serpent Mound, *Serpent Mound State Memorial, Ohio,* *October 1990*

from its mystical origins; we can only speculate about what ancient beliefs may have inspired its creation. Now, as in centuries past, the great snake lies coiled with power, tempting us all with its enigmatic presence.

Moose Mountain

WHEEL OF MYSTERY

The Moose Mountain Medicine Wheel is on top of a high hill just west of Moose Mountain Park in southeast Saskatchewan. This medicine wheel, perhaps the most complete example of the spoke-shaped stonework in Canada today, was built several centuries ago by North American Indians. Some of the spokes are thought to be in alignment with celestial events, but even the local Indian people admit that the original purpose of the medicine wheel has been lost, and they look forward to future investigations, which may help them understand its meaning.

When I photographed the central cairn of rocks in the predawn light, the silhouette reminded me of a sleeping giant, perhaps the profile of an old Indian chief. As I watched the morning light push back the stars, I wondered if the giant might slowly waken to reveal once more the mysteries of Moose Mountain.

Silhouette of central cairn and predawn sky, *Moose Mountain Medicine Wheel, Saskatchewan, June 1990*

Bighorn

WHEEL OF THE HEAVENS

Traced out in an intricate design of boulders, the Bighorn Medicine Wheel lies on a level ridge near a ten-thousand-foot (3,077 m) summit in Wyoming's Bighorn Mountains. Twenty-eight spokes are still clearly visible, reaching out from the central cairn of a near-perfect circle eighty feet (25 m) in diameter.

The placement of several other cairns on or near the circumference appears to be haphazard, but some archaeoastronomers believe they mark specific astronomical events. One cairn aligns perfectly to the point of sunrise at the summer solstice, and several other alignments indicate the risings of major stars.

Even more impressive to me than these links with the heavens is the location of this wheel on the earth. The Bighorn range rises dramatically from the surrounding flat plains that seem to stretch forever. I spent three days camped near the wheel, enjoying the spectacular vista from these lofty heights, and watching the parade of elk, deer, and the mountain sheep that give Bighorn its name. Little is known about the people who built this medicine wheel possibly as long as seven hundred years ago, but it stands today as a symbol of man's quest for a link to the heavens.

Bighorn Medicine Wheel, aerial view, Bighorn Mountains, Wyoming, September 1990

Canyon de Chelly

VALLEY OF HEALING

Arizona's Canyon de Chelly, in the northeast of the state, is a region of sublime natural beauty. Many of the canyon walls plunge a thousand feet (308 m) to the canyon floor, which was clothed during my visit in its summer greens of aspen, prickly pear, and the geometrical patches of corn planted by local Navajo Indians. The view from the canyon rim is one of spacious splendor, and also affords a chance to spot some of the dozens of cliff dwellings that cling precariously beneath the overhangs, as though built by ancient bird-people. This red-rock canyon is believed to have been a continuous place of pilgrimage since 300 AD, first by the Anasazi people, which means "ancient ones" in the Navajo language, and then, in the 1700s, by the Navajo.

My favorite among these unusual houses

White House ruins, Canyon de Chelly, Arizona, September 1990

was one known as the White House, located at the base of a sheer sandstone cliff-face displaying 200 million years of geological artwork. Although village life in the area reached its peak about eight hundred years ago, the site, unlike many others, has never been abandoned, and throughout the centuries the canyon region has maintained its reputation as a source of healing powers.

Chaco Canyon

BRIDGE TO THE SUPERNATURAL WORLD

Although the earliest buildings on the site date from 400 AD, the pueblos of Chaco Canyon in northwestern New Mexico were built around 900 AD by the Anasazi Indians. An extensive road network stretching more than two hundred miles (320 km) in all directions marks Chaco Canyon, during its heyday, as the crossroads and cultural center for a vast number of people.

The most unique feature of Anasazi building is the kiva, a large circular structure built partly underground, with stone-lined walls often interrupted by niches. Still in use today by contemporary native American groups, it is believed that the kiva was originally used, among other things, for religious ceremonies, sky watching, and initiation rituals. I was drawn to Casa Rinconada, where I photographed the night sky from this large ceremonial kiva, which resembles an open-air amphitheater. The two grand entrances into the kiva align perfectly with the North Star, shown in this photograph. Like the Egyptians and the megalithic builders of ancient Britain, the Anasazi seem to have constructed with a purpose, reaching out to the supernatural world and attempting to find meaning in the universe.

Casa Rinconada and star traces around Polaris, Chaco Canyon, New Mexico, September 1990

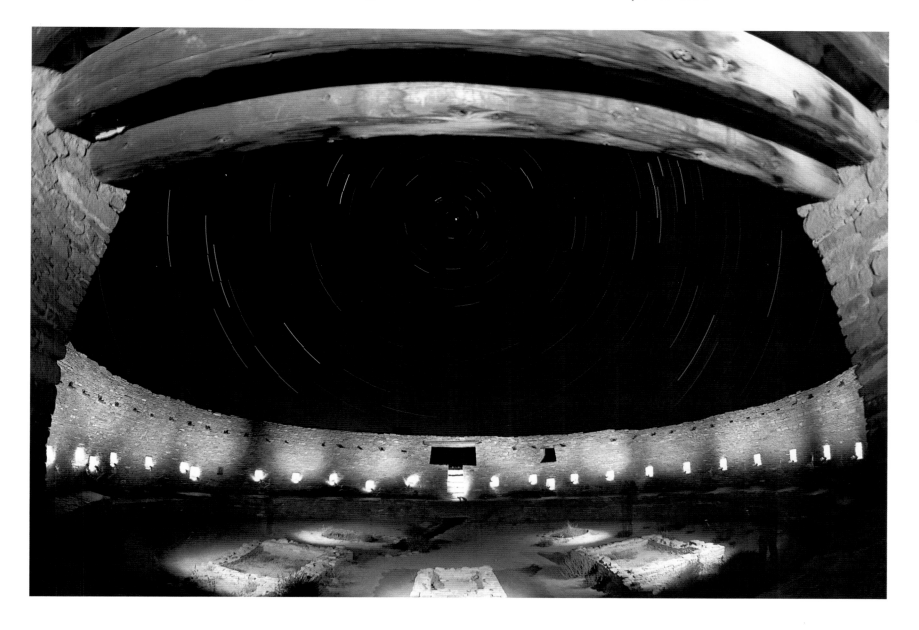

Ninstints

REALM OF TOTEM SPIRITS

Ninstints, on Anthony Island, lies to the southwest of Moresby in Canada's Queen Charlotte Islands off the coast of British Columbia. Nestled among the trees on the east shore of this tiny island, yet visible from the bay, is the largest grouping of totem poles in existence. Fifteen mortuary poles and three spotted deer were on hand to greet me when I arrived by water on a sunny July morning. For several minutes I simply sat in the boat, bathed in the perfection of this place most sacred to the Haida Indians, and now also revered the world over as a designated World Heritage Site. From a distance, I could barely make out the tracings of a raven, a killer whale, a beaver, and a bear in the worn and rotting wood.

The Haida believed that animals and birds, like people, had supernatural powers. The figures on the mortuary poles, erected only as a chief's or shaman's grave post, depict the animals most central to Haida religion and mythology. I felt great sympathy for these old totems—leaning, falling, and slowly dying—something I have never felt about stone carvings. Maybe it is because we share a common mortality. I felt a sadness meeting them for the first time in their old age, and yearned to have known them standing proudly in the clarity and strength of their youth.

Mortuary poles, Ninstints, Anthony Island, Queen Charlotte Islands, British Columbia, July 1982

Detail of mortuary pole, *Ninstints, Anthony*
Island, Queen Charlotte Islands, British
Columbia, July 1982

Golden Lotus

Lotus pond, Ubud, Bali,
Indonesia, June 1989

SPIRIT OF THE
SUPREME BEING

I was walking by a small carp pond in Ubud,
Bali, when I noticed the leaves of a lotus
plant catch the early morning light. When I
stood directly in line with the sun, the plant
was transformed into gold, and I was reminded of the Hindu creation mythology, in
which the supreme being is personified by a
golden lotus on a great sea.

Chapter Two

Waters of Cleansing

We live on a planet whose surface is nearly three-quarters covered by oceans, and whose continents are blessed with countless freshwater lakes. Beneath these land masses are further vast stores of life-giving waters that seep or gush to the surface in various forms—springs, rivers, pools, geysers, and waterfalls.

With our critical dependence on water to sustain life, it is little wonder that this element has been regarded as sacred throughout the course of human evolution; virtually every culture has ascribed spiritual powers to some or all of its waters. Many of these designations are unique, associated with mystical tales and wondrous mythologies, but some universal symbols do emerge. Flowing water, for example, is often associated with fertility and the eternal cycle of birth, death, and rebirth. And most cultures use water for ritual cleansing and for purification through baptism. The flow of a river may have double significance, traveling upstream representing a return to the source of one's being, while downstream symbolizes the course of life. Some rivers, the Nile and the Ganges, for example, have long been regarded symbolically as the lifeblood of their respective nations. Lakes often gain their sacredness from qualities of stillness and depth, lending themselves to legends of birth and creation. And many waters around the world are associated with healing powers.

Possibly because of the magnificent spectacle they present, waterfalls have frequently been the inspiration for dramatic myths and legends. My pilgrimage led to some of the most awe-inspiring waterfalls on earth, the trip to Angel Falls in the heart of the Venezuelan jungle being among the most dangerous and exhausting I have ever undertaken. Perhaps the element of risk, the commitment to the unknown, are part of what give some of these sacred places their hallowed sense of reverence. I was rewarded at Angel Falls with brilliant images, but even had I returned empty-handed, the falls would still hold their magic for me, perhaps maintaining a more potent spell, having evaded the best efforts of an ardent pilgrim.

Holy wells, springs, and waterfalls, sacred rivers, pools, and lakes have since time immemorial held an inherent fascination for mankind. Exploring sites from a variety of cultures around the world, this chapter offers an insight into the mysteries of earth's sacred waters.

Agua Azul

HOLY WATERS OF MEXICO

Surrounded by dense jungle in Mexico's Chiapas region, the waters of Agua Azul seem to appear out of nowhere, then gently tumble over rounded rocks. The falls mark the convergence of three rivers, which provide enough water for the cascades to be a showpiece even during the dry season. Though the largest fall is only about forty feet (12 m) high and fifty feet (16 m) wide, the succession of lacy waterfalls coursing over the uneven terrain is enormously captivating, and the desire to be a part of them quite compelling.

Upper falls, Agua Azul, Chiapas, Mexico, March 1988

Because the waters spread out so evenly and the slope is so gradual, many pilgrims commune with Agua Azul by climbing up through the shallow water, while others choose to dive from the lip of the lower drop into the tropical pool below. I paid my homage to Agua Azul, known also as Blue Water, simply by sitting under a tree on the bank and feeling the peace instilled in me by the blue and turquoise hues. Sometime later, I found Agua Azul on a list of the nine holy waters of the world.

Swimmers at lower falls, Agua Azul, Chiapas, Mexico, March 1988

Lake Wabby

ANCIENT WATERS OF
THE BUTCHALLA PEOPLE

In 1770 Captain Cook sighted Fraser Island, the world's largest sand island, off the coast of what is now Queensland in Australia. At one time this island, measuring about seventy-seven miles (120 km) long, was home to several hundred thousand of the Butchalla people. With the subsequent invasion by the white man, these people became almost extinct.

Because the waters surrounding the island are salt water, the Butchallas valued the inland fresh-water lakes such as the one shown here for drinking, cooking, and bathing. But I felt a certain sadness looking at the active sand dunes surrounding Lake Wabby, realizing that they are constantly shifting with the wind and in so doing, pushing this tiny island lake to its inevitable demise.

Lake Wabby, *Fraser Island,*
Australia, August 1989

Spring of Pan, Banias, Israel, January 1989

Banias

HEADWATERS OF THE JORDAN

A stone's throw from Pan's cave on the west slope of Israel's Mount Hermon is the Spring of Pan. Here, marking the ancient sacred city of Banias, the headwaters of the Jordan River erupt from the inner reaches of Mount Hermon to begin a 156-mile (250 km) journey southward to the Sea of Galilee and onward to the Dead Sea. Tradition associates the waters of the Jordan River with John's baptism of Christ, and it has further significance, according to the Book of Joshua, as the "one last river" that Joshua and the children of Israel had to cross in their deliverance to the Promised Land.

The spring, hidden under the cave, emerges into a series of adjoining pools, whose movement is still enough to reflect the evening light on the cliff face that contains the Cave of Pan. Like pages torn from the history of Biblical times, the autumn leaves have dropped from their branches to form a sheltering canopy over the sacred waters.

Spring of Daphne, *Mount Olympus, Greece, January 1989*

Spring of Daphne

HOME OF A GREEK TRAGEDY

Visiting the Spring of Daphne in the Vale of Tempe near Mount Olympus brings to mind one of the most tragic love affairs in Greek mythology, involving Daphne, a forest nymph of unequaled beauty, and Apollo, an eternally young and handsome warrior. After slaying the python at Delphi, Apollo foolishly taunted Cupid with his prowess; in revenge, Cupid shot Apollo with a golden arrow of love, and pierced Daphne with one made of lead, a love repellent. Weary of Apollo's advances, Daphne begged her father to destroy her beauty so she would be left alone. Obligingly, he turned her into a laurel tree and Apollo, still hopelessly in love, adopted the laurel as a sacred symbol.

When I visited the Vale of Tempe, I too
found grace and delicacy in the trees, albeit
denuded of their summer adornment.
Daphne's spirit hovered in the leafless forest,
stripped of its bright colors, teaching us to
appreciate the muted elegance that
surrounds us.

Woods beside Spring of Daphne,
Mount Olympus, Greece, January 1989

The Dead Sea

THE SEA OF LOT

Separating the present-day countries of Israel and Jordan is the Dead Sea, an extremely long narrow body of water southeast of Jerusalem. At 1,306 feet (400 m) below sea level, this salt-water lake marks the lowest terrain in the world. The heavy concentrations of salt allow one to float easily on its surface, and the unique mineral content, combined with the clean air, sunshine, mud pools, and hot springs, offers healing powers that attract pilgrims world-wide to its shores and spas.

The Dead Sea is associated with the wicked and decadent Old Testament city of Sodom, thought to have been located somewhere in the area. Before God destroyed the city, he warned Lot and his family to leave, but not to look back. Though Lot obeyed, his wife cast her eyes back on the burning city and was turned into a pillar of salt, and for centuries the sea was known as Bahr Lut, Arabic for Sea of Lot. In modern times, the lake acquired the name Dead Sea because, despite what are believed to be its healing

Dead Sea viewed from Masada,
Israel, December 1988

properties, no plants or animals can thrive in the high salt content of its water.

One afternoon I drove from Jerusalem to Masada, a rocky elevation just west of the Dead Sea, where in 73 AD, 960 Jews committed mass suicide rather than surrender to Roman soldiers. In the evening light I photographed the world's lowest landscape, capturing it perhaps as the Jewish martyrs would have seen it in the last moments of their time on earth.

Waikiki

SACRIFICIAL WATERS OF KU

Waikiki Beach is best known today as a world-famous holiday resort, with its white sand beaches, luxury hotels, and extravagant nightlife. But originally, Waikiki, which means "spouting water," was a special place of power for the ancient Hawaiians. Above the beach is Diamond Head, so named because sailors thought the sparkling crystals of the monolithic rock might be diamonds. In the shallow, richly colored waters below, King Kamehameha, from his fleet of war canoes, held lavish ceremonies in honor of the gods. When the war god, Ku, required appeasement, human sacrifices were hurled from the dizzying heights of Diamond Head to the rocks below.

Nowadays, the only ritual at Waikiki is the daily sacrifice of the flesh of thousands to the sun god, in the hope of returning to northern climes with skins as brown as the Hawaiians'.

Couple strolling on Waikiki Beach,
aerial view, Oahu, Hawaii, February 1987

Paliuli

EARTHLY PARADISE
OF THE GODS

In Hawaiian mythology, Paliuli is described as an enchanted garden, a lush land moist with springs and waterfalls, purposely hidden by the gods so they alone could partake of the waters of eternal life. One version describes it as the first land made by the gods, where they created earth's first man and woman. In this legend, the garden is located in the uplands of Ola'a, in the forest between Hilo and Puna on the Big Island of Hawaii.

My Paliuli experience was in a lowland rainforest on the coast near Hilo. When I came upon these falls glistening with cool spring water nestled beneath an overhang of banana and breadfruit trees, I was convinced I had found the Hawaiian Garden of Eden. I drank from the waters and partook of the fruits, and if the feast does not keep me eternally young, the experience at least left me with a vision of an earthly paradise I will not soon forget.

Falls at Hilo Botanical Gardens,
Big Island, Hawaii, February 1987

The Yangzi

RIVER OF THE IMMORTALS

The Yangzi River carves its way through central China for 3,237 miles (5,179 km), linking Sichuan Province with the eastern portions of the country. The third largest river in the world in terms of volume (after the Amazon and the Congo), it has served for centuries as a major trade route through the country and also provided access to the Pacific Ocean. But the Yangzi has also stood as a tangible link to immortality. Legend has it that the Immortals lurk in the moonlit early morning mists, sometimes flitting from one mountain to the next, or flying on the backs of storks. According to the Chinese with whom I shared a three-day boat trip, the Immortals can be sensed hiding in the river fog, but always disappear as you get closer. Not quite gods, but definitely enchanted beings, they are highly sought after since it is believed they hold the key to immortality. One emperor in the third century BC launched a major expedition to find the "islands in the eastern sea" that held the secret of eternal life. As I stood in the moist night air watching from the bow of our boat, I surmised that if the emperor had chosen to make his eastward voyage on the Yangzi, he would have found the hiding place of the Immortals long before reaching the Pacific.

Yangzi River in moonlight,
China, May 1989

Futami Rocks

SACRED BOND OF MARRIAGE

The Futami Rocks, Meoto Iwa in Japanese, also known as the Husband and Wife, or Married Rocks, lie in the sacred waters off the coast of Japan's Ise Shima National Park, a short distance from Ise city. According to ancient Shinto belief, these two rocks, symbolically joined in matrimony by an ornately braided rice-straw rope, are the incarnations of Izanagi and Izanami, creators of Japan. The torii gate atop the husband, Izanagi, indicates that the kami, or spirits, are keeping watch over the shrine. Once a year, on January 5, the rope is ritually renewed, another indication of the great importance of this couple to the Japanese, who try at least once in a lifetime to witness, as I did, the Married Rocks at sunrise.

Bird over torii gate, *Married Rocks, Futamigaura, Japan, April 1989*

The Married Rocks,
Futamigaura, Japan, April 1989

Shiraito Falls

WATER OF WHITE THREADS

Mount Fuji is so sacred to the Japanese that any waters flowing from its slopes are highly revered. Shiraito Falls, on the western lowlands of the mountain, beautifully illustrate the graceful "white threads" of their Japanese name, and are of special importance to the Shingon school of Japanese Buddhism. The monks meditate by standing under the main flow of water, sometimes without moving for hours at a time. When I was there in April, the runoff from the recently melted snows of Fuji's upper slopes was almost too cold to drink. Yet the two monks shown opposite waded into the pool at the base of the falls, clambered onto the wet rocks, and stood for forty minutes with hands pressed together, in honor of the Buddha in all of nature. In spite of my reluctance to emulate their method of worship, I marveled at how intimately they knew these holy waters, and how completely they were spiritually committed to the natural world.

Stream below Shiraito Falls,
Fuji-Hakone-Izu National Park, Japan,
April 1989

Shingon Buddhist monks at Shiraito Falls,
Fuji-Hakone-Izu National Park, Japan,
April 1989

Arike Pond

VISION OF HARMONY

Whether we seek solace in a Japanese garden or in the morning mists along the Nile, the quest is the same. Regardless of race, creed, or color, we tend to seek out places that bring harmony and balance to our lives.

In the Shinto gardens, the Japanese attempt to create a feeling of bliss through the use of harmonious shapes. When I sat by Arike Pond in Nara, the roundness of the rocks was echoed in the shape of the lotus leaves and also in the tiny round sakura petals. For a monk receiving inspiration from this scene, however, no such analysis is needed; indeed, it would simply get in the way of pure meditation.

Lotus and sakura petals,
Arike Pond, Nara, Japan, April 1989

The Nile

LIFEBLOOD OF
ANCIENT EGYPT

The Nile flows north through Egypt, passing the ancient city of Thebes, the valleys of the kings and queens, and the famous pyramids of Giza, before emptying into the Mediterranean Sea. Known today to be the world's longest river (4,132 mi/6,648 km), the Nile of ancient times was seen by the Egyptian people as the lifeblood of the country and the symbol of eternal life.

Hapi was the god of the Nile, a fertility symbol said to provide the annual, eagerly awaited floodwaters from his bottomless jar. So sacred was the river in the hearts of the people that it was seen as representing Nun, the primordial sea from which everything originated, and source of all nourishment, both physical and spiritual.

Dawn light on Nile River near Luxor,
Egypt, December 1988

Today the river is more subdued. The Aswan Dam, built in 1971, created Lake Nasser, the largest man-made lake in the world. And although the dam now controls the flow of water and provides year-round irrigation, it also prevents the annual flooding of the plains, which in earlier times provided precious, rich topsoil to the flatlands along the river's floodplain.

Sailing the waters of the Nile in a small
boat called a felucca, I saw no royal retinue
of barges, nor heard the sound of trumpets
at the gateway to Thebes, but the sun god,
Amun, still sparkles on its waters and
children squeal and wave from the banks; and
even though Hapi's jar may be cracked with
age, the river flows eternally.

West bank of Nile River near Luxor,
Egypt, December 1988

West bank of Nile River near Luxor,
Egypt, December 1988

Bodega Bay

CATHEDRAL OF SUNLIGHT

Bodega Bay, a short distance north of San Francisco on North America's Pacific coast, is blessed with spectacular surf, high cliffs, and spacious sandy beaches. Here, southern Californians make sojourns north in search of a smog-free, sun-filled sky, but also to find the quietude of empty beaches. Others, from the inland climates, are drawn west by the call of the sea, and receive the baptism of its spray.

As I peered through my viewfinder at the sinking sun mirrored by the wet sand of a receding wave, shown oppposite, I felt awed by the miracle of sunlight. Virtually every aboriginal culture has deified the sun, and all religions in some way symbolize divinity as being in "the light." Normally so bright that we cannot observe it directly, the sun here showed its true colors, a gift to all the children of the universe.

Sunset and mist, Bodega Bay, California, August 1988

Sunlight on wet sand,
Bodega Bay, California,
August 1988

The Pacific Rim

BACKBONE OF THE AMERICAS

The Pacific coast extends from the western tip of the Alaska Peninsula to Cape Horn, on the extreme tip of South America. Stretching twenty-five thousand miles (40,000 km) and rising to become the Coast, Rocky, and Andes mountains, this mighty shoreline, along which lies a chain of sacred sites, forms the unbroken backbone of two enormous continents. Scholars of geomancy, the study of earth energy, tell us that the Pacific coastline has many power points that have become places of pilgrimage for contemporary man—sites that have been known intuitively for centuries by native cultures along the coast.

With the color mauve being symbolic of the spiritual world, the haunting predawn light in this image of the Oregon coast seemed the perfect representation of the Pacific Rim and all the mysteries of its sacred sites.

Predawn light, Pacific Ocean, *Oregon coast, November 1987*

Emerald Lake

CALL OF THE YUKON

Emerald Lake is a colorful example of the sacred places that fall along the Pacific coast mountain chain. Located in the St. Elias Range, a short distance south of Whitehorse, Yukon, this tiny jewel of water many thousands of times smaller than the Pacific Ocean draws people to its shores with equal attraction. Aptly named for its blue-green appearance, Emerald Lake received its heavenly color from the fine mineral silt deposited during a glacial retreat. Long before man's frenzy for Yukon gold, these turquoise waters called the southern Tutchone Indians to its banks, where they worshipped the water as a manifestation of the Great Spirit that created all things, including the fish, the mainstay of their existence.

I have made several excursions to Emerald Lake. Each time the color is different, with unique variations in tone, but the ducks, muskrats, and other water creatures remain the same, marking their presence with delicate V-shapes on the glassy surface of the lake as they cruise along the shore of their home.

Emerald Lake, *near Whitehorse, Yukon, June 1987*

Quetico

SPIRIT OF GREAT BEAUTY

The Quetico Lake region in Ontario, Canada, sprawls over eighteen hundred square miles (4,660 km²) near the border of the United States, about halfway between Thunder Bay and Kenora. For centuries this hauntingly beautiful waterscape, now preserved as a provincial park, was home to the Ojibwa Indians. On a windless evening the waters seem to take on a spirit force, causing a characteristic ripple like that made by Windigo, the giant man-eating monster of Indian legends. Quetico, however, refers to the presence of a benevolent spirit typically found in places endowed with great natural beauty.

Only when I flew over the region, thirty thousand feet above the endless network of lakes, did I get a sense of the waters as living spirits, guardians of the Ojibwa world.

Quetico lakes, aerial view,
Quetico region, Ontario, August 1989

Niagara Falls

REMNANT OF THE ICE AGE

About twelve thousand years ago, the Niagara Escarpment was dominated by huge glaciers, pushing their way through gorges, forming cliffs, carving out channels, and creating the lakes and rivers that characterize the region today. One result of this gargantuan activity, which marked the end of the last ice age, was the formation of Niagara Falls, which attracts five million tourists a year from around the world. With the preponderance of resort hotels and nightly entertainment that encroach on its banks, one would not guess that Niagara Falls was a sacred place to the Indians two centuries ago, or that it appears on lists of the holy waters of the world.

To photograph Niagara Falls in its natural state without the intrusion of twentieth-

Spring buds on maple tree,
Niagara Falls, Ontario, April 1988

century civilization was a tough task. A long lens, however, permitted me to reach across the Niagara Gorge from the Canadian side and isolate an area of the American Falls, portraying the uncluttered majesty of a lost era.

The Everglades

ABODE OF DANGER

Spilling into the shallow lagoons of the Gulf of Mexico, the Everglades is a network of swampy waterways on the southern tip of Florida. Protected as a wildlife sanctuary, it is home to a myriad of bird and insect species, a hideaway for countless small mammals and water creatures, and domain of the ominous alligator, which moves in the water with a silent and sinister force, like an evil spirit that both horrifies and fascinates. Perhaps it is this duality of attraction and repulsion that draws modern-day explorers like a magnet to gaze into the murky depths.

Alligator, *Everglades National Park, Florida, January 1985*

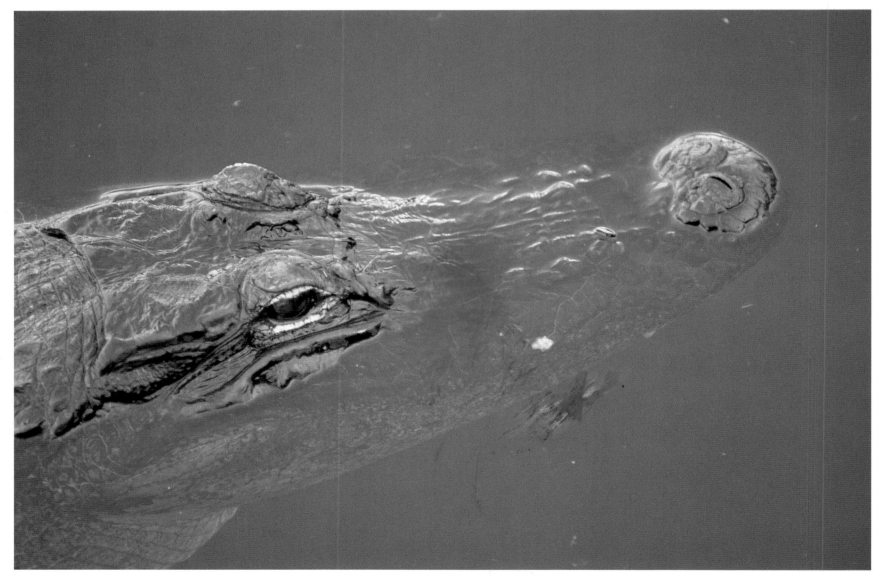

Galapagos

EVOLUTION OF THE SPIRIT

Galapagos is a Pacific archipelago dominated by thirteen large islands that straddle the equator six hundred miles (1,000 km) off the west coast of Ecuador. Here, almost a century and a half ago, Charles Darwin found the inspiration for his theory of evolution, which provided the world with a revolutionary version of creation. My four visits to the Galapagos Islands have been an on-going spiritual journey; they are a haven where I go not to solve the riddle, but to sense the mystery.

Leaning over the bowsprit with our cameras, my companions and I shared the pure cosmic energy as dolphins leapt into the sunlight. Seeing our reflections in the viewfinder, I felt like we were voyaging on a spaceship watched over by dolphin spirits.

Leaping porpoise and boat reflection,
Galapagos Islands, Ecuador, February 1985

The Rainbow

PATHWAY TO THE HEAVENS

The sacred waters of our planet are not always in the pools, lakes, streams, and rivers, but are sometimes found in the sky in the form of rainbows. Though the rainbow has many meanings to different cultures, I like to try and experience it according to the mythology of the people I am visiting. When I flew over the Hawaiian Islands, I could see the peaceful Pacific below me through a band of colors refracted by the plexiglass of the airplane window. As I photographed, using a polarizing filter to enhance the colorful effect, I was reminded that one Hawaiian legend believes the rainbow to be a bridge to the other world high in the sky. With the gods above and the earthly mortals below, only a chosen few were allowed on the pathway between. Looking through the rainbow from above, I indeed felt privileged.

Clouds and rainbow, aerial view, *Pacific Ocean near Hawaii, February 1987*

Lotus Pond

PLACE OF PURITY

I found this lotus pond in a corner of the pristine gardens at the Mahabodhi Temple in Bodhgaya, India, where Gautama Buddha walked and prayed following his enlightenment under the Bodhi Tree. Now a painted stone statue of the Buddha seated on a lotus oversees this sacred pond. As I peered down from the steps that lead to the water's edge, I could see him reflected among the lotus plants, as though the Buddha's spirit was keeping watch.

Some Buddhist sects speak of heaven as a sacred lake of lotuses, where the souls of the deceased, resting within the lotus buds, await admittance to paradise. The bud either flowers or wilts, depending upon how the individual lived during his lifetime. The lotus is usually seen as an emblem of purity because it is not of the earth, but rises without blemish from the waters.

Sacred Lake, Mahabodhi Temple,
Bodhgaya, India, February 1989

The Ganges

MOTHER RIVER OF INDIA

The Ganges River, India's most sacred waterway, rises in a cave in the Himalayas and flows south for 1,650 miles (2,640 km) to the Bay of Bengal. Its name comes from Ganga, the Hindu goddess of purification. One Indian myth speaks of the Ganges as the earthly continuation of the Milky Way. Though its holy waters are used to heal the sick, soothe the weary, cleanse the body, and for the immersion of the prayerful, the Ganges' greatest purpose is to transport the souls of the dead. There is no greater honor in India than to die beside the Mother Ganga and have one's ashes sprinkled over her waters. Consequently, many pilgrims come here to die, and thirty-five thousand bodies are cremated each year in the burning ghats at Varanasi, popularly known today as Benares, the holiest Hindu city in India.

I spent many hours rowing on the river at Varanasi, hoping to feel the holiness of this ancient place. But the diversity of activities, the range of color, the noise and confusion, and the sheer number of people was too overwhelming to absorb in a single visit. No sooner would I frame one scene in the viewfinder than another drama would emerge to tug at my consciousness.

Early morning is the time to experience the Ganges, to watch the silent mother goddess awaken from her slumbers, then to feel the quickening of her pulse as the ghats along her shores begin to fill with the teeming humanity of another day.

Woman in prayer, *Ganges River at Benares, India, February 1989*

Rising sun and Ganges River,
Benares, India, February 1989

Hindu pilgrim and Ganges River,
Benares, India, February 1989

Ganges River and bathing ghat,
Benares, India, February 1989

Air Panas

HOLY SPRING OF BATUKAU

On the gentle slopes of Mount Batukau on the island of Bali is a garden of exceptional beauty and grace. Air Panas is historically a holy spring and currently an important place of pilgrimage for the Hindu Bali people. Families converge here for the day to swim in the sacred pools, explore the harmonious blend of natural and man-made gardens, and picnic beside the sacred streams that emerge from the mountain.

"Why is this spring so sacred?" I asked a father watching over his three little ones immersed in the warm mineral water. "Because Batukau, the great spirit, lives here," he replied simply.

The god Batukau is so revered that every temple on the west side of Bali, which is dominated by the mountain that bears his name, has a shrine venerating his spirit. If the saturated colors of the gardens, the inviting gurgle of the springs, or the tropical aromas of the dense jungle were signs of his spirit, then I too experienced Batukau at home on his mountain.

Ti plants, gardens and spring,
Air Panas, Bali, Indonesia, June 1989

Ti plants, gardens and spring,
Air Panas, Bali, Indonesia, June 1989

Cape Kidnappers

PLACE OF THE RISING SUN

Cape Kidnappers is the farthest eastern tip of New Zealand and thus the place where the dawning sun can first be seen. For the Maori people, both the rising sun and the east were symbolic of the life force. Holy men in days gone by would face the rising sun during special rituals and ceremonies, and their houses would be built on the easternmost point of the village.

Although it was named by the explorer Captain Cook after the Maoris attempted to kidnap his interpreter, a young Tahitian boy, Cape Kidnappers is better known today as the largest Australasian gannet sanctuary in the world.

For several days I camped on the tip of the peninsula with twelve thousand gannets. Observing the colony and becoming familiar with the birds' behavior put me in touch with

Australasian gannets, Cape Kidnappers, New Zealand, October 1984

the special energy of the cape. The birds seemed undisturbed by my visit and we shared the space at a respectful distance, waking together at the first hint of eastern light.

Byron Bay

CATCHER OF FIRST LIGHT

Byron Bay extends to a rocky promontory in New South Wales, marking the extreme eastern tip of Australia. Geologically, the region is 20 million years old and is believed by some to channel electromagnetic earth energy to the summit of nearby Mount Warnung. The Aborigines were the first to recognize it as a special place, calling the mountain Wollumbin, which translates as "cloud catcher" or "weather maker." As with Cape Kidnappers on the opposite page, the Byron Bay area is significant to the Aboriginal peoples because it catches the first rays of the rising sun, symbolic of life, well-being, and happiness.

For me, the place of greatest natural energy was at water level, where the waves danced with an animation and vitality that seemed inspired by joy.

Breaking wave, Byron Bay, Australia, August 1989

The Amazon

Amazon River,
Brazil, February 1983

GATEWAY TO THE
PRIMORDIAL PAST

The Amazon River, greatest waterway on earth in terms of volume, trickles from the snow-capped peaks of the Peruvian Andes and is fed by eleven hundred tributaries on its way through the colossal Amazon Basin to complete its four-thousand-mile (6,400 km) journey to the Atlantic. Its proportions defy the imagination: two hundred miles (320 km) wide at the mouth, it drains an area of 2.5 million square miles (6.5 km²). In its swollen waters lurk piranhas, caymans, and the dreaded anaconda—or so adventure writers would have us believe. My journey down the Amazon in an enormous dugout canoe revealed a less dangerous though swiftly moving waterway. Diving from the gunwale of my canoe and bobbing like a cork in the mainstream, I let the river carry me for about an hour. Snakes and alligators, I found, were not a great threat.

Revered for centuries by the many jungle tribes that dwell along its banks, and honored for its size and might, the river now faces its greatest challenge: the onslaught of the industrialized world. If the Brazilian forests continue to be destroyed, the Amazon will become the drain of an eroded wasteland, and an unwitting accomplice to one of mankind's most heinous crimes against the planet.

Lake Titicaca

"THE WOMB OF MANKIND"

Lake Titicaca, the highest navigable lake in the world, borders the South American countries of Peru and Bolivia. This huge lake was revered by the ancient Incas as the birthplace of their world. Perhaps because of its ideal altitude, or maybe because of what are believed to be the life-enhancing powers of its water, Lake Titicaca today is thought to be a haven of longevity, the residents along its shores claiming to be among the oldest people on earth.

The refreshing air and the cooling offshore breezes offered a pleasant escape from the oppressive heat of the Peruvian lowlands. I remained in the city of Puno for several days and religiously rose each morning to greet the sunrise. Watching the sun emerge, seemingly from the depths of the lake, made it easy to imagine the origins of the Incan creation story, which told how everything, even the sun itself, was born of the waters.

Lake Titicaca shoreline near Copacabana,
Bolivia, December 1987

Angel Falls

Tulume Bena, now called Angel Falls, plummets 3,212 feet (988 m) from the north face of the massive Auyantepuy Mountain in the spectacular Canaima wilderness area of Venezuela. The existence of the falls was unknown to the outside world until 1935 when Jimmy Angel, a daredevil bush pilot from the United States, came upon them while searching for gold on the mountain. Prior to this, they were known locally as Big River Falls, and were long revered by the Kamara Cota Indians before the Spanish conquest of South America in the sixteenth century. In recent times, a hermit who has lived near the falls for forty years has attested to hearing haunting sounds of crying from the cliffs at night; he believes these are the voices of Inca gods. Others camped nearby claim to have heard an entire city of sounds high on the mountain.

Rainbow at base of falls, Canaima National Park, Venezuela, May 1990

Angel Falls (opposite), after heavy rain, Canaima National Park, Venezuela, May 1990

Even the river beneath Angel Falls seemed to move with a magic energy, its waters in many places taking on an astonishing bright red color that spelled power and vitality. Though minerals from the soil and the roots of the surrounding plants give the river its glow, I felt as if I were watching the lifeblood of the planet coursing through the arteries of mother earth.

Caruna River below Angel Falls,
Canaima National Park, Venezuela, May 1990

Akaka Falls

PRECIPICE OF GODLY GRIEF

I quivered, looking down into the semicircular chasm of Hawaii's Akaka Falls, realizing that the 420-foot (130 m) plummet could bring a decisive end to my life. Akaka Falls, north of Hilo on the east coast of the Big Island, is the site of a legendary tale about the god Akaka and his two charming mistresses, Lehua and Maile. Akaka fell to his death from the precipice above, and the falls that sprang from the face of the rock are believed to be the unquenchable tears of his ladies; unable to contain their grief, Lehua and Maile were transformed into the two smaller falls nearby.

When I spotted the brilliant red leaves of this ti plant juxtaposed against the falls, I found in them the perfect symbol of the passion and bloodshed that ended this tragic tale of love and woe.

Ti plant at Akaka Falls,
Big Island, Hawaii, February 1987

Haena Point

BIRTHPLACE OF THE HULA

The Hawaiian hula dance originated here at a temple called Kaulu Heiau, twenty-seven hundred feet (830 m) above the waters off Haena Point on Kauai's Na Pali Coast. In the beginning, the Hawaiians tell us, the god Laka came down to earth and taught men the hula as a form of worship during religious ceremonies. Later the dance was given to the women, who had to demonstrate their devotion to Laka by jumping from the temple heights into these swollen waters, and swimming to the safety of Kee Beach below.

Perhaps it is not coincidental, I mused as I photographed from the safety of a rocky point, that the fluid motions of the hula resemble the majestic rhythms of these waves. Like the dance, these waters also depict the soul of Hawaii in motion.

Breaking wave, *Haena Point,*
Na Pali Coast, Kauai, Hawaii, February 1987

Fan wave, Haena Point, Na Pali Coast, Kauai,
Hawaii, February 1987

Tel Dan

"THE GARDEN OF EDEN"

I always imagined the Garden of Eden to be a primordial jungle bursting with life. This Christian place of original sin would need to gush with waters, tempt with sensuous color, and exude a warm earthiness—a seductive place indeed. There is much disagreement among religious scholars as to the location of the garden; evolutionists, of course, question its very existence, but the idea of a place where man lived in harmony with the earth has been a powerful myth in many cultures. When I explored the Tel Dan Nature Reserve on the lower slopes of Mount Hermon in Israel, I felt that my quest for Eden had ended. This garden of gnarled thickets, rushing streams, and stately eucalyptus touched by a light breeze and anointed with bird song was my Paradise Lost.

Tel Dan Nature Reserve,
Israel, January 1989

Chapter Three

Havens of Renewal

Throughout the ages, earth's forests, jungles, gardens, caves, and other special secluded places have offered mankind shelter, protection, and an opportunity for physical and spiritual renewal. Each culture has marked its most sacred places as sanctuaries set apart from the commerce of daily life. Responses to these havens are as diverse as the geography in which they are found. Each is unique, each offering the pilgrim its own prescription for personal healing.

A haven may be as small as a seat beneath a shady tree or a cave just large enough to shelter one person. Or it may be as vast as a desert, defined only by the edges of its endless dunes. Sometimes the sense of freedom afforded by an expanse of open ground is as refreshing as the ambiance of a cloistered garden, the refuge from the madding crowds being more crucial to a revival of the spirit than protection from the elements.

The havens depicted here have been chosen to illustrate this enormous diversity. I have included a few well-known sites, such as the Garden of Eden, the Cave of Pan, and Avalon, places familiar to many because of references to them in religious texts or myths and legends. Others are the sanctuaries of a particular culture, like the deer parks and shrines of Japan, the thermal areas of New Zealand, or the forests and rocks of Australia. A few sites have become sacred for me personally as a result of my experiences there during my global wanderings.

We can learn much from exploring the sanctuaries that have sustained others through the centuries. More important, perhaps, is to use these places as points of reference for discovering havens of our own.

Eucalyptus bark detail,
Tel Dan Nature Reserve,
Israel, January 1989

Cave of Pan

SHEPHERD GOD OF BANIAS

On the southern slope of Mount Hermon in northern Israel there is a cave with rustic colorful walls. Since pre-Christian times it has been believed to be the home of Pan, a shaggy-haired deity of the wild countryside, who was half goat and half man. When I entered his spacious cave it was somewhat difficult to maneuver around the uneven floor, but not difficult to believe it was the dwelling place of a goat-footed god. The cave is located at Banias, a sacred city originally called Paneas in honor of Pan. Although there is a Roman influence evident in the archway carved on the cave's exterior, Pan's spirit can still be heard inside, a faint hint of musical notes, perhaps carried on the wind from a distant panpipe.

Cave of Pan, Banias, Israel, January 1989

Dieng Plateau

SPIRIT PLACE
OF THE HINDUS

One interpretation of the Javanese name Dieng is Spirit Place, a fitting description for the Dieng Plateau, which was a place of pilgrimage from the eighth to the twelfth century. Shrouded in mystery, this strange enchanting highland is hidden away about sixteen miles (26 km) from Wonosobo in central Java. For those who seek solitude to commune with nature, it offers many options: a forest, a meadow, a plateau, a thermal area that speaks in a sulfury language of erupting steam vents and bubbling pools, and several small Hindu temples that accent the landscape.

For me the most sacred place on the Dieng Plateau was Lake Warna, shown opposite, a quiet volcanic pond that often changes color, apparently reflecting the

Trees, Dieng Plateau,
Java, Indonesia, June 1989

mood of anyone who sits in reverie on its grassy banks. The plateau beckoned me to stay awhile and unwind, to absorb the many colors of its mineral-stained rocks, mosses, and trees, and to enjoy the light cooling rains.

Water and reeds, Lake Warna,
Dieng Plateau, Java, Indonesia, June 1989

Reed Flute Cave

CRYSTAL PALACE OF THE DRAGON KING

Discovered during the Tang Dynasty (618–906 AD), Reed Flute Cave, on the outskirts of Guilin, China, is famous for its beauty and its spacious rooms steeped in mystery and legend. Gateway to the exotic scenery of its famous mountains, Guilin ironically boasts some of its most spectacular landscapes underground. When I saw the stalactites and stalagmites mirrored in the stillness of the reflecting pool, above, I could hardly believe they were real, and it was only when the occasional droplet splashed on the perfect surface that the illusion was shattered.

The cave acquired its name from the reeds at its mouth, which are used by the locals to make small flutes, but some of the gigantic columns inside are more reminiscent of pipe

Reflecting pool, Reed Flute Cave, Guilin, China, April 1989

organs. The largest room, the Crystal Palace of the Dragon King, takes its name from the Chinese novel, *Journey to the West*. According to the story, the Dragon King fought the Monkey King, who used the dragon's own needle, a huge pillar in the center of the room, as a weapon to conquer his army of jellyfish and snails, now visible as petrified remains on the floor of the cave.

Basalt column,
Reed Flute Cave, Guilin,
China, April 1989

Wanjian Loo

BAMBOO GARDENS
OF CHENGDU

On the outskirts of the city of Chengdu in China's Sichuan province is a haven of peaceful solitude. Wanjian Loo, the River Viewing Pavilion Garden, has more than 120 varieties of bamboo adorning the landscape. Like many of China's bamboo gardens, it is reminiscent of the early imperial parks, where bamboo was planted as a Confucian symbol of the true gentleman. In the Taoist tradition, the bamboo represents man's inner strength; it is tall and strong, yet supple enough to bow in the wind.

It was relatively easy to document the stately stability of the bamboo at Wanjian Loo, but to depict its delicacy and its gentle

Bamboo abstract, Wanjian Loo Garden, Chengdu, China, May 1989

movement was a momentous challenge. By adding a color-refraction filter to my lens and overexposing the scene by two settings, I was able to make an image that conveyed for me the spirituality of this remarkable plant.

Autumn snowfall, aspen trees, near Saskatoon, Saskatchewan, September 1984

Aspen Grove

HAVEN OF THE PLAINS INDIAN

Though much of the Canadian prairie is predominantly flat and treeless, groves of aspen and birch thrive in the coulees and low-lying areas. As well as offering a haven for deer and many smaller mammals, these bluffs were sacred to the Indians. They provided shelter, poles to build tepees and travois, wood for weapons and utensils, fuel for ceremonial and cooking fires, and a place to commune with Gitchi Manitou, the Great Spirit. In the autumn these trees accent the prairie with brilliant splashes of color. But when the first snows arrive prematurely in mid-September, as shown in this image, the trees are dressed in their finest whites, a celebration of two seasons in one.

Prince Edward Island

"CRADLE IN THE WAVES"

Prince Edward Island, the smallest of Canada's ten provinces, has the largest rural population, with over 60 percent of its inhabitants living in the countryside. The Micmac Indians, who have lived in the area for two thousand years, called the island Abegweit, meaning "cradle in the waves," reflecting its gentle, pastoral qualities and also, perhaps, its facility to sustain abundant life.

Though famous for its fertile red soils, I was more attracted to the beaches and sandhills along the waterfront, with the smell of salt in the air and the warm summer winds providing a tangible link to the spirit of these maritime shores.

Queen Anne's lace and brown-eyed Susans,
east coast, Prince Edward Island, July 1984

Avalon

GATEWAY TO THE
SPIRIT REALM

Prior to my journey to Glastonbury, England, my impression of the mythical Isle of Avalon was of a place so full of spirit powers and romantic mystique that you could not be sure if you were in an earthly or heavenly realm. My visit affirmed that here the veil between the two is indeed thin. The veil, it seemed, had the same deceiving properties as glass: one instant I was looking through to another world, the fanciful kingdom of Arthur, of Celtic ghosts, Druid rituals, and quests for the Holy Grail. The next moment the glass became a mirror in which I saw myself, wide-eyed at the tourist tales, yet doubtful as to the ultimate meaning of it all. It somehow seemed fitting that the Celtic burial ground in the area was called Ynis Witrin, meaning Isle of Glass.

I had no idea how I would depict the essence of Avalon in a visual statement until I watched the mist begin to evaporate one

"Mists of Avalon," Glastonbury, England, August 1989

morning from the top of Glastonbury Tor. "There's the veil," I murmured. The drifting mist would occasionally reveal glimpses of an idyllic realm, which would then, just as suddenly, vanish.

Iona

ISLAND OF INCEPTION

A short distance off the west coast of Oban, Scotland, lies the tiny island of Iona. On the south shore is a pebble-strewn beach called Columba's Bay, which marks the arrival point of Celtic Christianity in Scotland, and the beginning of its spread throughout the British Isles. Sometime in the second half of the sixth century AD, Columba, a fiery Irish monk, went into self-imposed exile here after clashing with his colleagues at home. Landing on Iona, the story goes, he immediately climbed a hill and, discovering that he could still see his native Ireland, founded his abbey on the other side of the island, spreading the gospel with missionary zeal from a monastic community that would flourish for six hundred years.

Columba's Bay, *Island of Iona, Scotland, November 1988*

As I explored Columba's Beach, I found a rock with a niche containing a stone about the size and shape of an egg. I was drawn to it, fascinated by the notion of the egg symbolizing the beginning of a new life. I felt as if I had discovered the most sacred spot on the island.

Rock detail, Columba's Bay,
Island of Iona, Scotland, November 1988

Plymouth

SCENE OF THANKSGIVING

Although explorer Martin Frobisher celebrated Thanksgiving in 1578 in the eastern Arctic, the event observed by the Pilgrim Fathers at Plymouth, Massachusetts, in 1621 comes more commonly to mind when one thinks of the first Thanksgiving in North America. Following the Pilgrims' first harvest, Governor William Bradford invited the local Indians to join them in three days of festivities, a time for everyone to express gratitude for the bounties of the earth. Though celebrated sporadically over the next century and a half, Thanksgiving eventually became a national institution in both the United States and Canada, with the traditional meal of turkey and pumpkin pie acknowledging both the nourishing qualities of the land and the spirit of a common heritage.

My visit to Massachusetts at Thanksgiving time also resulted in a bounteous harvest, a visual feast of autumn color. As I focused on a swatch of fallen leaves against the black soil, opposite, I was reminded not only of the gifts of the earth, but also of the mysteries of the night sky. These leaves, perhaps the same variety that adorned the horn of plenty on the first Thanksgiving table, appeared to me as a depiction of the endless galaxies of the universe, a symbol of eternity.

Autumn foliage, *pincherry bush, Plymouth, Massachusetts, November 1983*

"Night Sky," *fallen leaves of aspen, maple,*
and pincherry, Plymouth, Massachusetts,
November 1983

Preacher's Cave

CATHEDRAL OF THE
NEW WORLD

In the autumn of 1647, the Eleutheran
Adventurers, English Puritans escaping from
religious persecution in Massachusetts,
landed on one of the Bahama islands off the
east coast of Florida. Their ship ran aground
on a reef and they sought shelter in a large
coral cave a short distance from shore. They
called their new island home Eleuthera,
which is Greek for "free"; the name has
lasted to the present day. On the first Sunday
of their arrival, the locals told me, a sermon
was preached from a pulpit-shaped rock at
the mouth of the cave.

Salvaging one small ship, a few brave souls
made the journey back to New England for
supplies to establish a colony. "To avoid the
foul sin of ingratitude," they later repaid
those who had helped them by contributing
to a fund for the institution that eventually
became Harvard University.

Preacher's Cave, *Eleuthera Island,*
Bahamas, January 1986

Preacher's Cave (exterior),
Eleuthera Island, Bahamas, January 1986

Red spruce at sunset,
Rockport, Maine, July 1979

Rockport

MEMORIES OF YESTERYEAR

Little imagination is required to see the early American colonists making good use of the east coast timber—cabins, furniture, wagons, and ships quickly depleted the forests. And they did not stop to consider the consequences of felling the trees that surrounded them; there seemed to be an endless supply. But in a few short decades virtually all the stands of usable lumber had disappeared from the east coast of the United States. When I found this small grove of red spruce near the town of Rockport, Maine, I was awed by its simple beauty, yet saddened by the reminder that it was but a token of what had once been the American wilderness.

Mystery Rocks, West Block,
Cypress Hills Provincial Park,
Saskatchewan, August 1981

Mystery Rocks

ENIGMA OF THE CYPRESS HILLS

The Cypress Hills, straddling the southernmost border between Alberta and Saskatchewan, rise to the highest elevation of land in Canada east of the Rockies. Near the summit, on a level plateau, is a configuration of rocks almost perfectly carved into enormous cubes. I was mystified and intrigued as I scanned the uniform geometry for the first time. So precise are the fractures and so ordered are the blocks that I swore they must be the handiwork of an ancient but technologically advanced culture, perhaps the foundation of some mighty temple. Those who are inclined to less spiritual interpretations claim that the formations were shaped by natural forces, a splintering activity as the bedrock settled in prehistoric times. In either case, there are several small hollows carved into the top, possible evidence that this may have been a ceremonial site for the Indians of the region.

Paine

JEWEL OF PATAGONIA

At the extreme southern tip of the Andes Mountains in Chile lies a land of enchantment called Paine National Park. Towering over seven thousand feet (2,300 m) above the surrounding hills, the Cuernos, sculpted brown-capped peaks, loom as a surrealistic centerpiece to the area. Here the excessive winds, known as the katabatics, can blow destructively and relentlessly for days or weeks.

In contrast to the hellish summits, the green hills and valleys below provide a place of refuge. As the mists evaporate from the lowlands, the jewels of the Patagonian landscape are unveiled, revealing a paradise for those seeking mystical encounters. Rich with a palette of hauntingly beautiful colors, the Cuernos are visible from almost every

The Cuernos, Paine National Park, Chile, February 1988

vantage point, a continual reminder that although heaven may appear to be at the top of the mountains, in Patagonia one should seek it in the protected beauty of the valleys.

"Old Man Spirit"

GREAT ROCK OF GREY GLACIER

There is a massive protrusion of granite between the two immense arms of Grey Glacier that reach down to embrace Lago Grey in Chile's Paine National Park. In this stone, carved by nature and painted by the minerals of millennia of ice flows, there sits what appears to be the bust of a wise old man with the wrinkled hide of an elephant and a long pointed nose. He never moves, yet he appears to see all and know all. Though I may be the only one to have found this knowing face at Grey Glacier, his presence is manifested in many forms of nature; here, he seemed to me a kind of guardian spirit of the place. When I sat at his feet in silence, I imagined him speaking to me with the wisdom of the ages.

*"**Old Man Spirit**," rock, Grey Glacier, Paine National Park, Chile, February 1988*

Antarctica

LAST BASTION OF WILDERNESS

As one of the last essentially untouched land masses on earth, Antarctica has become a symbol not only of endangered species but also of threatened habitat. The krill, so important in the food chain that supports the seals, penguins, and whales, are being fished out in a race by several countries to establish themselves in the area. Unsightly oil drums lie rusting at the research bases, some encroaching on the penguin rookeries, while tourist boats and fishermen throw cans, bottles, and diesel fuel into the waters. Most significant, perhaps, is that high above its awesome snow fields there is a hole in the upper atmosphere known as the ozone layer, through which dangerous solar radiation is leaking. Antarctica has taught us the fragility of our mother planet; we should heed the message and take the opportunity it offers for us to mend our ways.

Gentoo penguin and chick,
Paradise Bay, Antarctica, January 1988

Hudson Bay

GATEWAY TO THE ARCTIC

Though polar opposites, the Arctic and Antarctic regions have much in common. Both hold a vast potential for development, but both remain largely untouched because of their harsh climates and relative inaccessibility. But with modern advancement in communications and technology, and in-creased demands for resources, the world is beginning to turn to these last frontiers.

In the past two centuries of growth, mankind has had the sense to set aside prescribed places—parks and areas of natural beauty or sacred significance—as havens of retreat from the industrialized world. Now we are faced with another challenge: to preserve areas large enough to maintain a semblance of what our planet was like before the industrial age. As I gazed out over the spring ice packs on Hudson Bay, I felt some reassurance that the Arctic and the Antarctic are still relatively unspoiled. With past experience, global cooperation, and judicious planning, we should be able to maintain the pristine wilderness of these areas for eternity.

Pack ice at sunset, Hudson Bay, Churchill, Manitoba, June 1985

Khutzeymateen

VALLEY OF THE GRIZZLY

Just north of Prince Rupert, on Canada's west coast, lies a valley of uncommon beauty. It is sacred to the Clayoquot Indians, who named it Khutzeymateen, which means "where bear and fish meet." Each autumn the salmon return to the Khutzeymateen River to spawn, drawing the grizzly and black bears out onto the estuary in search of an easy catch.

Now the entire valley and its wildlife, which includes about sixty grizzlies, are being threatened by the logging industry. We, the bear's only predator, and only friend, will determine the fate of both it and the valley as conservationists and corporations vie for control. We must consider our native peoples' reverence for the land and find the will to designate and protect havens that are sacred to us all.

Khutzeymateen Valley,
British Columbia, June 1990

Deadfall, *Khutzeymateen Valley,*
British Columbia, June 1990

Wikaninnish

HOUSE OF THE SALMON PEOPLE

Wikaninnish Beach lies on the west coast of Vancouver Island in British Columbia's Pacific Rim National Park. For hundreds of years the Nootka Indians have lived in this region, hunting and fishing for their livelihood. They believed that the salmon, an important component of their physical and spiritual sustenance, lived in human form in a large house under the sea. With the magical powers of gods, these salmon people could don scaled robes and transform themselves into fish. The Nootka showed great care and respect for their fish-brothers, washing the leftover bones and returning them to the sea, where they awaited new clothing and new life.

Wikaninnish Beach, Pacific Rim *National Park, Vancouver Island, British Columbia, September 1983*

As I made these photographs in the late-afternoon smoky haze of some inland forest fire, the land, the sea, and the sky seemed to blend into one. I was reminded of the world of the Nootka, who saw themselves as part of a mystical force that bonded all nature together, making little distinction between the natural features—the sea, the forest, and the mountains—and themselves. The spirit world was present in every aspect of their lives, thus all of life was a ceremony.

Wikaninnish Beach, Pacific Rim National Park, British Columbia, September 1983

The Great Sand Hills

SYMBOL OF TIMELESSNESS

One of Saskatchewan's best-kept secrets is a large expanse of sand dunes northwest of Swift Current. The hills are covered with cedar and sage, and poplar groves in the valleys provide shelter for mule deer, antelope, porcupine, rabbit, and other small mammals. On the western edge, extending the length of the hills, is a range of active dunes, bare of foliage, and continually shifting under the relentless pressure of the prevailing winds. Here, I feel spiritually at home. I am at peace, camping beneath a cloudless sky full of stars and northern lights, and waking to witness the magic of another dawn spectacular.

Dawn light, *Great Sand Hills, Saskatchewan, June 1986*

By day I roam and photograph, sometimes wandering for hours without seeing a single trace of the twentieth century. It is an idyllic world: unhurried, timeless, and untroubled. The blowing dunes gradually drift into the mind and the landscape blurs as in a dream.

Wadi Mousa

GATEWAY TO THE PROMISED LAND

Wadi Mousa is a vast rugged area in south-central Jordan that lies on a major rift zone running for more than 250 miles (400 km) through the center of the country. Mousa is Arabic for Moses, the name of the valley coming from the Old Testament story of Moses leading the Israelites from Egypt through the desert to the Promised Land. Here, at Wadi Mousa, Moses is said to have struck the rock with his staff, bringing forth water for all to quench their thirst.

I felt a certain awe standing on the ground where such momentous events are reputed to have occurred, but the desert does not need these associations to be regarded as a spiritual place. Since ancient times the desert has inspired a sense of mysticism, and only those who honor its sanctity will survive its rigors.

Wadi Mousa (Moses' Valley),
Jordan, December 1988

"Spirit Ridge"

THE FACE OF A GOD

Far from the commerce of our present-day world, somewhere in the northern reaches of the Canadian woods, Wakan Tanka, Great Spirit of the Indians, still lives and breathes. His heartbeat can be heard in the ripple of the aspen, his footsteps in the crackle of dry autumn leaves, and his voice in the haunting cry of the loon. I even felt I had found a likeness of his face carved in a great mass of rock, a personal place of pilgrimage for me, which I have called Spirit Ridge. The carving, measuring about sixteen feet (5 m) high, has been sculpted by the creative powers of the wind, and has probably stood there for centuries. Although the location is so remote that it would be virtually impossible to chance upon it, I choose to keep it secret, and in doing so, will assure that the carving remains undisturbed.

*"**Spirit Ridge**," sandstone cliff, northern Canada, August 1978*

Honaka'a

FOREST OF THE SPIRITS

I found these shapes on the trunk of a large eucalyptus tree near the small town of Honaka'a on the island of Hawaii. I was reminded how the ancient Hawaiians, like the North American Indians, believed that there were spirits in trees, rocks, rivers, caves, and the sky. I wondered, as I photographed the designs in the bark, if their legends and stories all came from great historic events, or if, like me, they enjoyed envisioning mythological characters painted by nature.

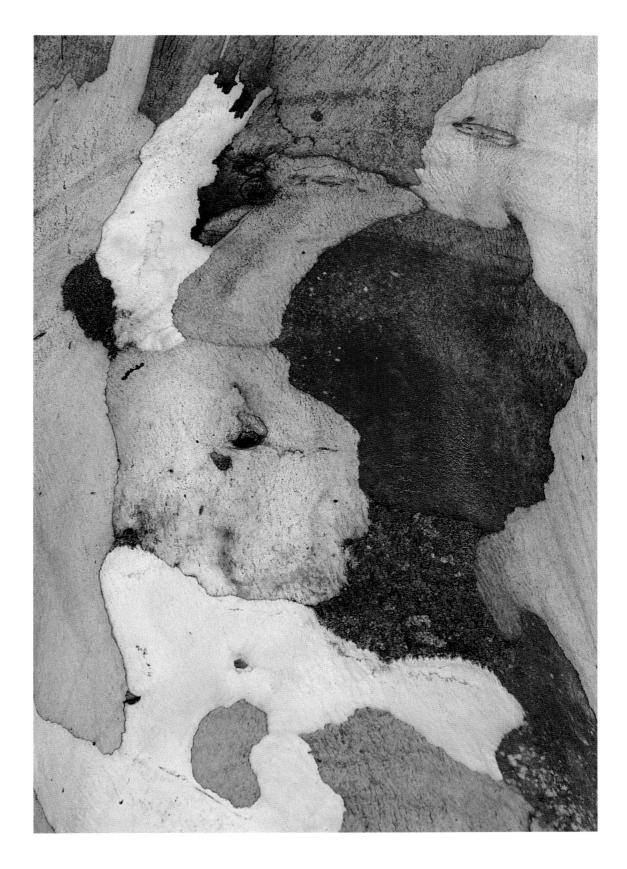

Eucalyptus bark, near Honaka'a, Big Island, Hawaii, February 1987

Lava Tree Park

ABODE OF THE SACRED OHIA

During one of the early eruptions of Kilauea on the island of Hawaii, a river of molten lava destroyed everything in its path except for a group of ohia trees, huge moist hardwoods able to resist incineration long enough for the lava to harden around their trunks. The trees eventually burned due to the internal heat of the lava, leaving a forest of solidified lava cones. The ohia trees are a tribute to the gods, and when in flower are so sacred to the Hawaiians that no one on the way to visit the volcano would dare pluck the brilliant red flowers or leaves. But when the volcano comes to the ohia trees, their sanctity is clearly violated.

Lava Tree Park, in the southeast corner of the island, is designated for the preservation of these unique statues. I felt I was walking among spirits. Each tree has its own peculiar

Lava Tree State Park,
Big Island, Hawaii, February 1987

size, shape, and character, and seemed to move behind my back in a prankish gesture to deceive me. Perhaps it was Pele, the fire goddess, displaying her powers over Hina-ulu-ohia, goddess of the ohia forest.

Waimea Canyon

MEETING PLACE
OF THE GODS

Waimea Canyon, over half a mile (1,000 m) deep and ten miles (16 km) long, was carved by the Waimea River on the Hawaiian island of Kauai. Known as the Grand Canyon of the Pacific, its purple, russet, pink, and red strata attest to the geological epochs over which this apparently limitless chasm was sculpted. Despite the desert-like conditions in the canyon area, there is a mountainous region in the center of the island that is the wettest place on earth, receiving over five hundred inches (1,250 cm) of rain per year.

Perhaps because the canyon is almost always in mist, it has acquired mythic and legendary associations. One story revealed to me by a local Polynesian was that the gods convened here in the canyon to plot the island's future. Though I did not hear the

Waimea Canyon, sunset light, *Kauai, Hawaii, February 1987*

whispers of the gods during my visit, I did come away replenished and uplifted by the haunting blend of color that paraded before my eyes.

The Sacred Valley

INCAN SOURCE OF ABUNDANCE

To the Incas, whose lives were steeped in worship, everything surrounding them was sacred. This Sacred Valley, a short distance from the Peruvian holy city of Cuzco, the former Inca capital, could have received its name for several reasons. The climate was ideal, its plains fertile, and its proximity to Cuzco made the bounty from its fields easily accessible. Furthermore, the valley is on the route to the jungle, which provided tropical fruits as well as the all-important cocoa leaf, used to induce heightened mental and spiritual states for festivals and ceremonial occasions.

The day I journeyed to the valley there were no fruit-laden caravans and no sacred ceremonies. But the sun god did appear to bathe the valley in a heavenly glow that left me feeling renewed after my sojourn in this special place.

Sacred Valley, *near Cuzco, Peru, December 1988*

Nourlangie

LEGENDARY ROCK OF KAKADU

Nourlangie Rock, an enormous sandstone outcropping, is one of the most prominent landmarks of northern Australia's Kakadu National Park. For thousands of years, this massive monolith has been a sacred place to the Warramal, the local Aboriginal people.

Its sheer size—over three hundred feet (100 m) high—its black and orange stripes, and its numerous fissures, caverns, and caves are impressive enough, but it is also famous for the abundance of its rock art and as the site of an Aboriginal legend from the time of the earth's creation, known as the Dreamtime.

It is said that two mythical Dreamtime creatures, a brother and sister, stole away to the top of the great outcropping, where they became lovers. As punishment for this transgression, she was banished forever from Nourlangie, and he was turned into a pinnacle of stone, which can still be seen from certain vantage points, jutting from the top of the rock. Though I found the legendary pinnacle, I felt more attracted to Nourlangie's eastern face, shown here, bathed in the warm glow of the day's first sunlight.

Nourlangie Rock, *Kakadu National Park, Australia, July 1989*

Kakadu

FOREST OF THE GAGADJU RITUAL

Kakadu is a vast national park bordering the north coast of Australia. Traveling one evening toward Ubirr, the most northern destination, I was astonished to drive past an area of the forest that was burning, apparently without any attempt by the park rangers to control it. Later I learned that the Gagadju, the local Aboriginal people who have lived in the area for at least twenty-three thousand years, regularly request the park service to burn the land in a complex, carefully timed patchwork fashion, in accordance with ancient customs and beliefs. In addition to creating a variety of habitats in which different plants and animals can thrive, this ritual burning also helps prevent wild forest fires, promotes new growth, and attracts new game to the area, all necessary for the survival of the Gagadju people and of the land itself.

Forest fire, Kakadu National Park, Northern Territory, Australia, July 1989

In the same tradition as the Gagadju, the Aborigines of Fraser Island off Australia's east coast also burn their waterfront property. Retaining the wisdom of their ancestors, these people understand intimately the food chain that is affected by the fires, and know the season, weather, and moisture conditions that will produce the most beneficial result. I photographed this moonlight torching from a safe distance on the beach. By morning, the fire had spent itself in the dewy stillness of the predawn, and birds were already flocking to the area to begin a thorough scavenging for small reptiles, insects, and rodents uprooted by the flames.

Bush fire and moon,
Fraser Island, Australia, August 1989

Calcarius thermal spring deposits,
Orakei Korako thermal area, near Rotorua,
New Zealand, October 1984

Ruatapu cave (left),
Orakei Korako thermal area, near Rotorua,
New Zealand, October 1984

Ruatapu

BIRTHING CAVE OF
ORAKEI KORAKO

A short distance from Rotorua, on the North Island of New Zealand, is Orakei Korako, a thermal area sacred to the Maori since before the arrival of the Europeans. Orakei Korako was one of several popular spots for bathing, and the more than two hundred hot pools were also used for cooking food, which was lowered in baskets. Though the entire area of geysers, mineral waters, and steam vents was a sacred place, the most revered feature was a cave called Ruatapu (shown opposite), which means "sacred pit." Only Maori women were allowed entrance; it was a private place of adornment, the small mineral pool at the bottom mirroring their beauty as they bathed. In addition, Ruatapu served as a secluded place of worship and as a birthing cave. Known also as Aladdin's Cave, it is a magical place decorated with nature's finest rock color, and has only recently been opened to the general public.

Rotorua

MAORI WATERS
OF CEREMONY

Rotorua, on New Zealand's North Island, is
an area of vigorous thermal activity that
begins at the Bay of Plenty, about forty miles
(64 km) to the east and continues to the
lower slopes of Tongariro in the southwest.
One Maori legend refers to Rotorua as the
Promised Land, where the original Maori
settled after migrating from a homeland
called Hawaiki. Lake Rotorua and the five
hundred hot springs in the immediate area
became sacred waters for these early settlers,
and every community had its holy stream or
pool in which to perform cleansing rituals.

I spent several days at Rotorua immersing
myself not in the waters, but in the Maori
culture. It was a joyous time, learning their
legends through song and dance, and photographing the mineral lakes, which were as
colorful and animated as the Maori
themselves.

"Artist's Palette," *Waiotapu thermal area,*
Rotorua, New Zealand, October 1984

Minichinas

VALLEY OF THE
VISION QUEST

To the northeast of Saskatoon, Saskatchewan, an extensive range of hills called the Minichinas stretches for fifty miles (80 km) on a north-south axis between Batoche and St. Denis. Though much of the land today has been broken by the plow, there are many gullies, ravines, and sheltered glades that still look as they did in the days when Cree and Ojibwa Indians camped here. It was to secluded spots such as these that Indian warriors would venture alone to find direction from the Great Spirit. Fasting and praying, sometimes for several days, the Indian would search for a sign that would affirm his life's pathway. These vision quest sites were identified as places of supernatural power, but today the locations of all but a few are unknown.

One morning in April, sitting alone in a grove of trees, I looked up and saw a red-tailed hawk trace an arc through the mists above. For many native Indian tribes, the hawk was a symbol of power; hawk medicine taught them to be aware of omens, visions, or messages from the Spirit. Seeing the hawk through the trees, I felt a privileged observer of a symbol sacred to countless generations of Plains Indians.

"Freedom," Red-tailed hawk and box elders, Minichinas Hills, Saskatchewan, April 1986

Antelope Canyon

CORRIDOR OF RAINBOW LIGHT

Antelope Canyon wends its way for about two miles (3.2 km) down to Lake Powell, near Page, Arizona. At its upper end the canyon narrows, at some places so tightly that you can leap across the top, yet it is more than two hundred feet (62 m) deep. On a sunny day the light bounces down the fissure, diminishing as it reaches the canyon floor, bathing the sandstone in a rainbow of colors and ricocheting into a golden glow across the walls, an effect that often lasts for only a few seconds. In the wet season, the canyon is largely inaccessible except for a short distance in from each end; the middle is restricted by deep pools and sheer vertical cliff faces.

A local Navajo Indian, who single-handedly lowered me by rope into a blocked central chamber, confirmed that Antelope Canyon had been sacred to his ancestors, but said he was not allowed to talk about its secrets. Placing my life in his strong hands and sliding into the abyss, I pondered what rituals might have occurred here when the indigenous peoples were the only inhabitants of the land.

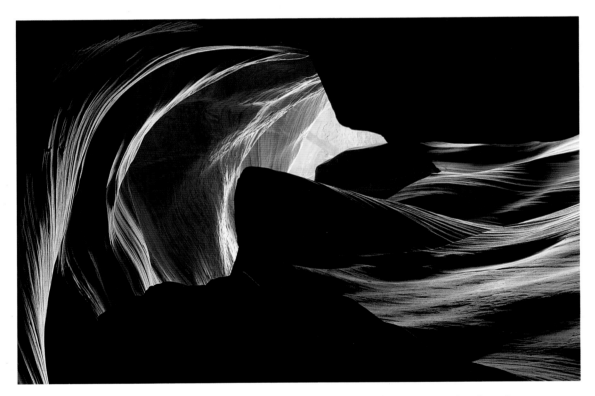

Sandstone formations, Antelope Canyon, Page, Arizona, September 1990

Sandstone arches (right), Antelope Canyon, Page, Arizona, September 1990

Valle de la Luna

VALLEY OF THE MOON

The Valley of the Moon in northern Chile is a wasteland of crusted volcanic rock extending over about thirty-five square miles (90 km²). After three hours encapsulated in a taxi hurtling through the dark of night, I did indeed feel as though I had arrived on the moon. Left to my solitary wanderings for the better part of a day, I experienced the exhilaration of total isolation, a limitless landscape, and a stillness so overpowering my breathing seemed intrusive.

As the light of a new day flooded across the valley, I followed a ridge for several miles, and making my way with some difficulty across the uneven terrain, I saw what appeared to be a road leading to a castle with chalk-white turrets. The piercing cold of night had turned to oven heat, and I wondered whether I was hallucinating or witnessing a mirage. In fact, it was neither—merely more of the volcanic rock sculpted by the wind, reaching up as though grasping for the heavens.

For me, a quality that signals the sacredness of any landscape is its power to engage the imagination. Here in this unearthly place I sensed a clarity of vision, a silence uncluttered by thought, and the assurance that a white castle awaited at road's end.

Volcanic ash flow,
Valley of the Moon, Chile, May 1990

Saltstone formations,
Valley of the Moon, Chile, May 1990

Valley of Longevity,
near Vilcabamba, Ecuador, March 1986

Vilcabamba

VALLEY OF LONGEVITY

In the spring of 1986 I made a pilgrimage to the southernmost reaches of the Ecuadorian Andes. Here, hidden away from the mainstream of the twentieth century, lies a valley with magical power. Vilcabamba, the Valley of Longevity, offers not only a haven of renewal, but the ultimate gift of long life. Its inhabitants claim that they live to become the oldest people on the planet. The secret is in the trees. Vilcabamba is the Spanish mispronunciation of Whelcapampa, Valley of the Whelca Tree. This miraculous tree, found only in and around this valley, produces particularly rich oxygen, charging the very atmosphere with health-giving properties. And high on a nearby mountainside is a sacred spring to which pilgrims come from around the globe. The stories of the miracles that have occurred at this spring parallel those during the time of Jesus. Some come to live in Vilcabamba simply to remain healthy, and visitors leave feeling one step closer to attaining immortality.

Shrine and camellia petals,
Byakugoji Temple, Nara, Japan, April 1989

Byakugoji

VILLA GARDEN
OF THE PRINCE

In Nara, Japan, I visited the Byakugoji, a temple founded in 715 AD by Gonso, a Shinto priest. This quiet corner of Nara, protected by majestic stands of bamboo, is nestled on a hillside, like many other Japa-nese shrines and temple gardens. It was originally part of a villa built for Shiki-no-miko, son of Emperor Tenchi.

Though the gardens extended over a sizable area, I found myself drawn to a small stone monument standing alone under a camellia tree. I might not have noticed it had the tree not bequeathed it with a carpet of petals. Here was testimony to the ideals of the Shinto faith, the perfect blending of artwork fashioned by man and nature.

Yoshino

HILLSIDE OF BLOSSOMS

Directly south of Nara is Mount Yoshino, site of Japan's most effusive display of cherry blossoms. Unlike most areas, the sakura here last for a full month because of the variety of trees and the variance in altitude at which they occur. A hundred thousand cherry trees cascade down the slopes in combinations of white, rose, pink, and red, dazzling the eyes of the viewer. Yoshino is a place of pilgrimage, especially during the month of April, when the blossoms grace the temples and shrines found mainly on the lower slopes. Seeing the hillside ablaze with color, it was easy to understand why the cherry blossom is believed to bring happiness and hope, and why it symbolizes the very essence of a Japanese spring.

Sakura trees, Yoshino Mountain, Japan, April 1989

Simono Senbon

FOOT OF THE MOUNTAIN

Sakura tree and fallen petals,
Yoshino Mountain, Japan, April 1989

For the Japanese, Yoshino represents the stages of a pilgrimage. Each portion of the mountain has a special significance. On the lower slopes, called Simono Senbon, are the first sakura to blossom each spring. The trail leads upward to Nakano Senbon, the midst of the mountain, and finally to the summit, or Kamino Senbon. The soul of Yoshino is in the depth of the mountain, Okuno Senbon, which can be experienced by visiting the sakura in all its manifestations. For me, Yoshino's soul felt most evident at Simono Senbon, a quiet nook beside a stream, where the sakura petals fell gently from the trees to adorn the water and the earth below.

Bahji Gardens

"PLACE OF DELIGHT"

To the four million Baha'is around the world, the gardens at Bahji, near Akka, Israel, are one of the most holy places of the faith. The extensive gardens surround the tomb of Baha'u'llah, founder of the faith, who was interred here on the day of his death, May 29, 1892. Though not a member of the Baha'i faith, I was permitted to enter the shrine and pay my respects in the modest building containing his tomb. Just as I was returning to the garden, I noticed a single orange that had dropped from its tree. It seemed so small lying alone on the great sweep of lawn, yet it served as a focus for the entire garden, drawing me into its lush, yet well-kept grounds. I thought it fitting that the original word for Bahji was Bahja, meaning "place of delight."

Baha'i Gardens at Bahji,
near Akka, Israel, January 1989

Date palm and salvia, *Baha'i Gardens*
at Bahji, near Akka, Israel, January 1989

The Lotus Temple

BAHA'I GARDENS OF INDIA

Completed in 1980, the Baha'i Temple in New Delhi, India, is one of the most unique structures in the world. The building is in the shape of a giant lotus, a symbol of harmony, purity, and truth. Each day the temple and its gardens attract thousands of visitors from all cultures and religions, a living testimony to its purpose of bringing together all peoples in one brotherhood. The founder of the faith, Baha'u'llah, believed that earth is but one country and mankind its citizens, and that since all people are manifestations of one God, and all parts of the globe are interconnected, human rights and world ecology must be addressed together.

During my visit to the Lotus Temple, I sensed the fruition of these truths as I watched the interplay of mankind and nature, with Baha'i, Moslem, Hindu, Christian, Buddhist, and Jew expressing equal delight in the beauty of the gardens, and partaking, for a time at least, of this harmonious blending of the family of man.

Lotus Temple, Baha'i Gardens, New Delhi, India, March 1989

Petunias, *Baha'i Gardens,*
New Delhi, India, March 1989

Fujisan

MOUNTAIN OF
EVERLASTING LIFE

Fujisan, or Mount Fuji, is the largest and
most sacred of all Japan's 265 volcanic
peaks, rising above the city of Fuji-Yoshida,
southwest of Tokyo. Named for Fuchi,
goddess of fire, by the early Ainu people,
Fujisan has not erupted since 1707. According to legend, Sengen-Sama, Shinto goddess
of the brightly shining blossoms, floats in the
form of a luminous cloud over the famous
peak. As I viewed Fujisan from the north,
Sengen-Sama was present, performing her
task magnificently.

Though the delicacy and grace of the
mountain can be admired from any distance,
it is customary for the Japanese, indeed the
duty of the faithful, to make pilgrimage to
Fuji at least once in a lifetime. Consequently,
three or four thousand people begin the
climb each dawn during the summer when
the pathway is open.

Fujisan (Mount Fuji) and sakura branches,
Japan, April 1989

Chapter Four
The High Places

❀

The high places on the earth—the mountains, volcanoes, certain hills, and natural monolithic rock formations—have long been held sacred by indigenous peoples around the world. Elevated well above the plane of everyday life, they offered a link between the material and the spirit worlds, and were often regarded as stepping-stones to heaven. These are bastions of often fearsome power and grandeur, and pilgrims to the temples, shrines, and sanctuaries on these high places believed themselves as close to their gods as earthly existence would allow.

On my treks to the high places I try to keep my eyes and ears open, partly to be in tune with the elements, and partly to hear the local stories that elucidate the omnipotence of the heights. Some indigenous people will not climb these mountains because of their fear or awe of the resident spirits. And other mountains are believed to be so sacred even recreational climbers will not ascend to the summit out of respect for the holiness of the peak. In the case of Mount Fuji, however, the most sacred of Japan's volcanic peaks, it is the duty of the faithful to make pilgrimage to the summit at least once in a lifetime. And in some cultures, that of the ancient Polynesians who settled in the Hawaiian Islands, for example, the sacred high places belong not just to the mountains and volcanoes, but to the sky, which was home to their creator god.

We visited a number of high places in chapter one, "Legacies from Antiquity," since man has often expressed his veneration for them by erecting such things as monuments, temples, sacred cities, or medicine wheels on high points of land. But just as frequently, earth's sacred high places are unmarked by the hand of man. Reverence for their natural beauty and the power and inspiration felt there have combined to maintain the mysterious and irresistible allure of their splendid isolation.

According to Japanese tradition, all the waters flowing from Mount Fuji are sacred. Thus, when I found this buttress of exposed rock anointed with spring waters trickling from the melting snows above, I felt I had discovered a special sacred place. Perhaps a key difference between a photographic journey and a conventional pilgrimage is in the focus. Whereas the entire mountain is revered by the Japanese, I was drawn to those views blessed with divine light.

Spring runoff on pahoehoe lava,
Mount Fuji, Japan, April 1989

As I photographed these swans on Lake Yamanaka, I wondered if the Japanese found the graceful shape of the swan's wings as inspiring as the slopes they mirrored on Mount Fuji. Certainly they were as white, and Shinto belief does assert that all creatures are an embodiment of a kami spirit. Meditating on the mountain's perfect symmetry reflected in the lake, I contemplated the English translation of Mount Fuji's name—Everlasting Life.

Swans on Lake Yamanaka and Mount Fuji,
Japan, April 1989

Mount Hiei

MOUNTAIN OF MANY PATHS

Mount Hiei, an ancient center of Japanese Buddhism, lies to the northeast of Kyoto, the capital of Japan at the time the monastery on its slopes was founded in 788 AD by a young man named Saicho. The central building of the restored monastery now stands on the site where Saicho originally built the small structure that he called Mount Hiei Temple, which housed his precious carving of the Buddha of Healing. Three lamps, known as the "inextinguishable Dharma Lights," have been burning ceaselessly in front of the main altar for over twelve hundred years. Saicho later introduced the Tendai school of Buddhism into Japan, which taught that just as there are many trails up the mountain, so too are there many paths to enlightenment, depending on one's level of spiritual development. My path on Mount Hiei took me away from the main group of temples to higher ground, where I found this row of monuments covered with lichen and moss. No signposts directed me to this sacred spot; an internal compass seemed to lead me to this place of solitude and peace.

Shrines near summit of Mount Hiei,
Japan, April 1989

Detail of shrine with lichen,
Mount Hiei, Japan, April 1989

Emeishan

"SUMMIT OF TEN
THOUSAND BUDDHAS"

Mount Emei lies in the south of China's Sichuan Province, rising over ten thousand feet (3,077 m) above sea level. It is one of the nine sacred mountains of China, four of which are sites of Buddhist pilgrimage. Standing at the top of this immense precipice, scene of countless pilgrimages over the centuries, I realized how aptly named was the peak—"Summit of Ten Thousand Buddhas." And as I gazed down at the specks of humanity below, I tried to imagine what this arduous climb must mean to the Buddhist pilgrims who might have traveled from the far reaches of China, Tibet, or Nepal. The final paces to the summit, with the spectacular view of the plain from whence they had been delivered, must seem like an arrival at the very gates of paradise.

One morning during my stay on the summit, the mountain was blessed with a light dusting of snow. It not only turned the landscape into a heavenly place, but clearly separated it from the lower slopes. But the fiercely cold fog banks that obliterated the view and clutched me in an icy embrace were reminder enough that as close to nirvana as this mountain top might aspire, it was also part of earth's grim realities.

Summit temple in mist,
Emeishan (Mount Emei), China, May 1989

Basalt columns, *Golden Summit,*
Mount Emei, China, May 1989

Guilin

DOMES OF INSPIRATION

Among the Guilin Mountains that surround the fern-shrouded Li River Valley of southern China, I sensed a harmony in all the elements of nature and a peaceful coexistence of man with the natural world. So complete was the synthesis, I felt I had walked into a painting. Indeed, these karst formations have attracted artists and poets for thousands of years; Guilin is so famous as an inspiration to creativity that these stylized peaks have become synonymous with Chinese landscape painting.

As the sun dropped between the peaks one evening in early May, the smoke from a nearby campfire brought ethereal light to the ferns, shown opposite, along the banks of

Farmer tending rice paddy, and Guilin karst formations near Yangshou, China, May 1989

the Li River at Xing Ping. The scene reminded me that the Taoist strives to find unity with all living things. Here was the perfect blending of the sensual, material, and spiritual worlds.

Karst formations and ferns,
Xing Ping, China, May 1989

Watching this sunrise from a shrine perched at the peak of a karst dome at Yang-shou, I felt as though I were witnessing a birthing. The very mountains seemed to open up, releasing the sun to a new life.

Karst formations and rising sun,
Yangshou, China, May 1989

Kane

"EYEBALL OF THE SUN"

In some cultures, the sacred high places belong to the sky. For the ancient Polynesians who settled in the Hawaiian Islands, the heavens were home of Kane, their creator god. They saw the universe as divided into three parts: upper heaven, realm of the gods; lower heaven, just above the earth; and earth itself, the garden of mankind. Lower heaven joined earth to upper heaven in a cloudland where visits to the gods were often made.

One afternoon as I was traveling along the south shore of Oahu, a puzzling shape emerged in the clouds. Then I saw the red sun staring at me and I remembered that one of Kane's manifestations was Ka-onohi-o-ka-la, or "eyeball of the sun." "Is that you, Kane?" I whispered, feeling a little self-conscious. As I photographed, I recalled an evocative phrase from Hawaiian lore: "when the wind whips the air, . . . when thunder peals without rain," then the god will appear "at the border of the heavens."

"Spirit of Kane," *cloud formation and sun, Oahu, Hawaii, February 1987*

Kilauea

CAULDRON OF THE
FIRE GODDESS

Kilauea is the most active volcano in the
world, an enormous caldera on the side of
Mauna Loa, the largest mountain on the island
of Hawaii. To the ancient Hawaiians, Kilauea
was the lava palace of Pele, goddess of fire, and
she retains her power in the eyes of the contemporary population, alluring many with the
glory of her flames and bringing death and
destruction to everything in her path.

Molten crust of lava lake,
Kilauea volcano, Big Island, Hawaii,
January 1987

Pele's reputation as an exquisitely beautiful but malicious temptress precedes the reality of her present destructiveness by many hundreds of years. One legend tells how only the spear of Lono, forged by a benevolent god, can reveal her true nature. When the tip is held to Pele's chin, her sinister countenance is illuminated. Like so many before me, I too was attracted by the brightness of her dress, the warmth and excitement of her fiery charms. On four occasions I flew over Kilauea in a helicopter, watching Pele hurl her tongues of flame into lakes of molten lava that flowed into the rivers of fire like great serpents crawling down the mountainside.

Dragon pattern on lava lake,
Kilauea volcano, Big Island, Hawaii,
January 1987

Once I gazed down into a 2000°F (1079°C) furnace where the collapsed roof of a lava tube revealed a Niagara Falls of molten lava. The searing heat was unbearable and the sound a thunderous roar. Such experiences made me realize that the earth's surface is but a crust—that we inhabit the solidified fringe of a fireball. Our well-being, indeed our very existence, depends ultimately on the whim of the fiery goddess and how much vengeance she chooses to ignite.

Lava tube from the air,
Kilauea volcano, Big Island, Hawaii,
January 1987

Uluru

CROSSROADS OF THE DREAMTIME

Ayers Rock—Uluru to the Aborigines—is the world's largest monolith, thrusting itself from the desert floor two hundred miles (320 km) southwest of Alice Springs in the center of Australia. Aboriginal settlements in the Northern Territory date back forty thousand years, establishing Uluru as the oldest known continuously worshipped site on the planet.

Despite the harsh conditions that prevail in Australia's central desert, my time at Uluru brought me an overpowering sense of peace and attunement to the ever-changing spectacle of this sandstone rock. For the early peoples, Uluru provided shade, protection, wildlife, and water from its springs and pools. But it gave much more than physical amenities. To know its importance is to understand the significance of all landforms to the Aboriginal peoples. Each tree, cave, lake, rock, in fact each geographic feature, was seen, and still is, as the embodiment of a spiritual event, some so sacred that they cannot be photographed or even visited by non-Aboriginals. In essence, the entire landscape is their Bible, and as such, all of nature is sacred.

Detail of sandstone wall,
sunset light, Uluru (Ayers Rock), Australia,
July 1989

In the beginning, referred to as the Dreaming or the Dreamtime, the Ancestors, huge half-animal and half-human mythical beings, roamed the desert forming trails upon which important events took place. Uluru lies at the crossroads of several of these trails, and thus is associated with a number of Dreamtime stories, which have been passed down through an oral tradition of song, ritual, and dance. Many ceremonies take place at sacred sites around the rock; these are exclusive to the local Aborigines and are only accessible to initiated people. Although visitors are allowed to climb one pathway to the top of Uluru, many (including Aborigines) choose not to climb, out of respect for this sacred area.

Ayers Rock has become an important earth symbol with newly emerging mythologies, and it is visited by increasing numbers of non-Aborigines each year. Its power, however, lies in the unbroken chain of Aboriginal worshippers stretching back into the mists of time.

North wall at sunset, *Uluru (Ayers Rock), Australia, July 1989*

Kantju cave (right), *Uluru (Ayers Rock), Australia, July 1989*

Kata Tjuta

CATHEDRAL OF THE ABORIGINES

Kata Tjuta, meaning "many heads," lies just west of Ayers Rock (Uluru) in central Australia. Known as the Olga Mountains to the recently arrived Europeans, Kata Tjuta consists of thirty-six domes spreading over about fourteen square miles (35 km²). The highest,

Mount Olga, was named after Queen Olga of Spain, who sponsored the first European exploration of the area in 1872. Geologists believe that at one time the domes may have been joined into one massive formation larger than Uluru today.

As at Uluru, many places at Kata Tjuta are associated with the sacred events of the Dreamtime, and are therefore off-limits to all but the initiated. There are other restrictions as well: much of the area, for example, may not be portrayed in paintings or photographs. In spite of the limitations, however, I found

Kata Tjuta much to my liking. The ambient light glowing among the canyons blessed the conglomerate walls with a warmth I have seldom witnessed. I remained in Mount Olga Gorge caught in a dream world of my own until the colors deepened and the darkness warned of the impending realities of night.

Olga Gorge, Kata Tjuta
(Olga Mountains), Australia, July 1989

Olga Gorge, Kata Tjuta
(Olga Mountains), Australia, July 1989

Lightning Dreaming

BATTLEGROUND OF DREAMTIME WARRIORS

Lightning Dreaming lies in Australia's Northern Territory, high on the crest of a cliff-faced escarpment on the eastern rim of Kakadu National Park. Because it is a dangerous sacred place for the Aboriginal people of this area, and hence to be avoided by everyone but the shaman himself, I photographed it from a distance. The site was a battleground of the Lightning Brothers, giant Dreamtime warriors. One story relates how the elder brother, in revenge for sexual transgressions against his wife, decapitated his younger sibling with a blow from his stone axe that struck with the force of lightning.

Lightning Dreaming from Nourlangie Rock, *Kakadu National Park, Australia, July 1989*

Archaeologists have suggested that around sixty-five hundred years ago the Australian climate changed dramatically, bringing on the wet seasons that were characterized by lightning storms. It was at this time that the spirit of Namarrkun, the Lightning Man, began to show up in rock paintings.

Gunung Batur

LEGEND OF FIRE

Bali, a small enchanted island in the Indonesian archipelago, is home to four sacred mountains: Agung, Batur, Abang, and Batukau. One evening I witnessed a moon-rise and lightning storm above Gunung Batur, which reminded me of the power of Lightning Dreaming on the opposite page. Despite its sacred qualities, Batur is regarded as equally dangerous by the Balinese. In 1917, one thousand people were killed and twenty-five hundred temples destroyed when a deluge of molten lava hurtled down the mountainside—a vengeful act, it was believed, by the goddess who lives at the summit. Some years later she struck again, destroying all but the highest shrine on the

Lightning and moon over Gunung Batur, Bali, Indonesia, June 1989

mountain. Photographing from a safe distance, I wondered, as moon myths are common in many cultures, if the full moon was believed responsible for igniting the fiery temper of the goddess.

Gunung Agung

THRONE OF THE DEITIES

Although each of Bali's sacred mountains is revered by the Hindu-Balinese, Agung, the largest, is most venerated of all. It dominates the landscape and is the site of the holiest of the many Balinese temples, Pura Besakih, the spires of which can be seen in the photograph on this page.

Gunung Agung is the throne of the Hindu deities and a place of pilgrimage for the whole island. Its history is steeped in mystery, its landscape accented with shrines in honor of the gods who anoint the surrounding villages with peace and prosperity. But, like Batur on the previous page, the spirit of Agung has at times also attacked with a vengeance. In 1963 the mountain erupted, destroying a fifth of the island. Many looked upon the devastation as a chastisement for offending the gods.

My visit to Agung was filled with a sense of bliss, in which I felt a protective spirit that gave me relief from the oppressive heat of the lower altitudes. The day I photographed at Besakih Temple, the mists came and went throughout the afternoon, suffusing the mountainside with an aura of enchantment.

Besakih Temple, *Gunung Agung,*
Bali, Indonesia, June 1989

Mount Semeru

VOLCANO OF HELLFIRE

From the lookout on the rim of Bromo Crater I could see the twelve-thousand-foot (3,692 m) summit of Mount Semeru to the southeast, expelling its dense clouds of smoke at thirty- to forty-minute intervals. The

Mount Semeru,
Java, Indonesia, June 1989

mystical appearance of this mountain reminded me of the legendary Mount Meru of the Hindus, a mountain thousands of miles in height with its base in hell and its summit in the heavens. Recalling my terrifying experience looking down into the volcanic heart of Kilauea in Hawaii, I could certainly believe that the boiling cauldron of Semeru was the no man's land between heaven and hell.

Bromo

NAME OF GOD

Mount Bromo, in the high country of Java, contains a crater within a crater. The larger one is rimmed by steep cliffs and spreads to a diameter of more than seven miles (11 km), encompassing the volcanic peaks of mounts Batok, Kursi, and Bromo, three somewhat attached mounds thrusting up from the crater floor. The smaller crater within the peak of Mount Bromo continuously belches sulfurous gases that leave brilliant yellow stains at the base, shown opposite.

East Java is the old land of the Hindu kingdoms, with Mount Bromo being home to the gods. Bromo is an Anglicization of Brahma, the supreme god of the Hindu trinity, and Bromo Crater has long been a place of pilgrimage where the faithful come in droves for holy days. Even as I stood at the lip of the volcano, I could see evidence of where local Tenggerese villagers had made offerings of fruit and flowers to the god of fire.

Bromo Crater Lookout,
Java, Indonesia, June 1989

Sulfur deposits and steam vents,
Bromo Crater, Java, Indonesia, June 1989

View at Bromo Crater Lookout,
Java, Indonesia, June 1989

Haleakala

"HOUSE OF THE SUN"

During my one-day trek across a section of Haleakala Crater on Hawaii's island of Maui, I glanced over a ridge to see both sun and mist playing on the gentle pastels of the crater floor. It reminded me of a lost city lying in rubble, a place full of mystic tales and romantic memories. Perhaps it was the atmosphere created by these soft muted colors that prompted the ancient Hawaiians to call it the "Land of the Living Gods."

Haleakala, in Polynesian, means "house of the sun." And Haleakala Crater does indeed reach closer to the sun than any other point on the island. At ten thousand feet (3,077 m) above sea level, Haleakala stretches for nineteen square miles (49 km²)—one of the largest craters in the world—and although it has not erupted since 1790, the volcano is not dead, but merely sleeping.

Mists on floor of Haleakala Crater,
Maui, Hawaii, February 1987

One of the legends associated with the crater concerns Maui, a mythical figure after whom the island was named. Some versions say he didn't have enough daylight hours for fishing; others say that his mother's laundry couldn't dry before nightfall. In either case, Maui lay in wait and, with a rope woven from coconut fibers, lassoed the sun's rays as they peeked over the rim of the crater. He kept the sun tied up until it promised to travel more slowly across the heavens. Whether or not Maui was successful, Haleakala's enormous moonscape remains the home of the sun as well as the mists, the rain, the fog, and the clouds.

Mineral deposits, *Haleakala Crater,*
Maui, Hawaii, February 1987

Morning mist, *Haleakala Crater,*
Maui, Hawaii, February 1987

Emerald Lakes, Mount Tongariro,
New Zealand, October 1984

Tongariro

HOME OF THE MAORI SPIRITS

Tongariro is a massive mountain rising to two peaks, Tongariro and Ngauruhoe, both with active volcanic craters, in the center of New Zealand's North Island. To the Maoris, the native people of New Zealand, Tongariro, along with many other mountains, is tapu, which means "sacred." Fairies and spirits are reputed to dwell in the mists obscuring the mountain's higher reaches, and close to the summit live evil spirits that sometimes rain fire and wrath upon the land. The larger the mountain, the more dread and veneration it inspires, and Tongariro is the greatest. One local tribe has buried its nobility on the mountainside for generations, further enhancing its sacred qualities. They believe, in fact, that Tongariro itself is one of their ancestors.

Not so long ago, few would have dared to infringe upon the sacredness of the summit, or risked their lives by climbing to the top. But, respectful of its spiritual attributes, I set out alone on foot for three days to experience Tongariro. I wanted to reach the saddle between the two peaks, where the crater is still active and where strange shapes seem to lurk in the mists. After climbing steeply through spring snows and layers of cloud, I did indeed find myself in a fairyland. Here, far beyond the tree line, were the Emerald Lakes, with Red Crater hugging the slopes above. Had the ancient Maoris dared to venture to these heights, the revelations would have confirmed their tales of a high sacred place, though one far more benevolent than the legends might suggest.

Red Crater, *Mount Tongariro, New Zealand, October 1984*

The Himalayas

"ABODE OF THE GODS"

Himalayas means "abode of the gods" in Sanskrit, and this massive range straddling Nepal and Tibet is sacred to Hindus and Buddhists alike. Their myths speak of Mount Meru, a peak said to be in the Himalayas, which stood at the center of the earth; it was peopled by gods and the cosmos revolved around it.

During my ten-day trek in the Himalayas, every bend in the trail would reveal a new and glorious vista. "There, surely, is Meru," I said to myself a dozen times. But when I arrived back at Pokhara I refuted all previous claims. Standing on the crest of the hill overlooking a vast expanse of Himalayan peaks, I swore this must have been the spot that infused pilgrims with the mountains' sacred qualities. As I stood rapt in the same awe and wonder that has inspired generations of travelers before me, I felt, once again, that our mother planet, in her finest moments, can cut through the petty distinctions of culture and religion and put all who are open in touch with the great beyond.

Mount Machupachare from Pokhara,
Nepal, March 1989

Everest

"MOTHER GODDESS
OF THE SNOWS"

The highest mountain on earth, at 29,028 feet (8,848 m), Mount Everest reigns over the Himalayas in the northeast corner of Nepal. To the Nepalese herdsmen who eke out a living on Everest's lower slopes, she is Chomo Lungma, which translates as "mother goddess of the snows." Whether attempting a climb or tending goats below the snow line, these Sherpas who know Everest are as respectful as they are reverent of her many moods. She first yielded to Edmund Hillary and Tenzing Norkay, who reached the "Summit Of Heaven" on May 29, 1953. One climber, attempting an ascent, summarized it as follows: "You never conquer Everest; at best you tread cautiously for brief periods when she allows you to."

I did not feel compelled to climb this mountain, but was content to photograph from the air, witnessing one of the most awesome spectacles on the face of the planet.

Mount Everest from the air,
Nepal, March 1989

Safed

HILLTOP OF HEBREW MYSTICISM

Northwest of the Sea of Galilee in present-day Israel lies Mount Canaan, mentioned in the Old Testament. Safed, high on the mountain's southern slopes, is the place where sixteenth-century Jewish scholars retreated to live holy, contemplative lives and to write what have become sacred texts for the Jewish faith. Based on a mystical interpretation of the Scriptures, their writings were known as the Kabbalah.

As I edged my way up the mountain, great vistas opened to the south, and as the evening approached, the mountain ridges reflected a new warmth and the clouds parted to admit a radiant light. I was reminded that the Kabbalah was based on the notion that the hidden God makes himself known through the imagery of light. I smiled as I photographed, imagining that this same view from Mount Canaan might have inspired these early mystics to sense the divine and write about it.

Hills in sunset light near Safed,
Israel, January 1989

Meteora

HERMITAGE ON THE ROCKS

High on the crest of a series of detached vertical rock formations near Kalambaka in northern Greece lie the ruins of thirteen monasteries called Meteora. When Meteora flourished, from the fourteenth to the eighteenth century, the buildings were virtually inaccessible except by rope ladders that could be hauled up at a moment's notice in case of emergency. The lofty perches on these colossal pillars of stone were chosen not for their proximity to God, but for their safety features. The original community of ascetic hermits lived in caves and later built shelters on the rock domes for refuge.

Today most of the buildings have deteriorated and are unsafe, but several have survived, maintained by a handful of Byzantine monks and nuns, and are open to the public. A paved road now winds upward to these monasteries and secure bridges have replaced the precarious ladders. I marveled

Monastery, *Meteora, Greece, January 1989*

at the spectacular views and thoroughly enjoyed the storybook charm as the tinkling of sheep bells echoed through the valley.

The Alps

HEART OF EUROPE

The Alps, a high and rugged mountain range, dominate the landscape of Switzerland and Austria, and also border on Italy, France, Germany, Hungary, and Yugoslavia. As I flew over, I was captivated by the serpentine shapes of the rivers, each glimmering briefly as it caught the morning sun. At the heart of Europe, the rivers rising in these mighty mountains carry life-giving waters to hundreds of cities, towns, and villages across the continent. Most notable, the Rhône and the Rhine flow northward, the Durance into the Mediterranean, the Adda to the Adriatic Sea, and the Dunarea eastward to the Black Sea. The Alps have been known as sacred mountains to climbers through the ages, and these misty slopes continue to cast a spell that draws visitors from around the globe.

The Alps, aerial view over Switzerland, *February 1989*

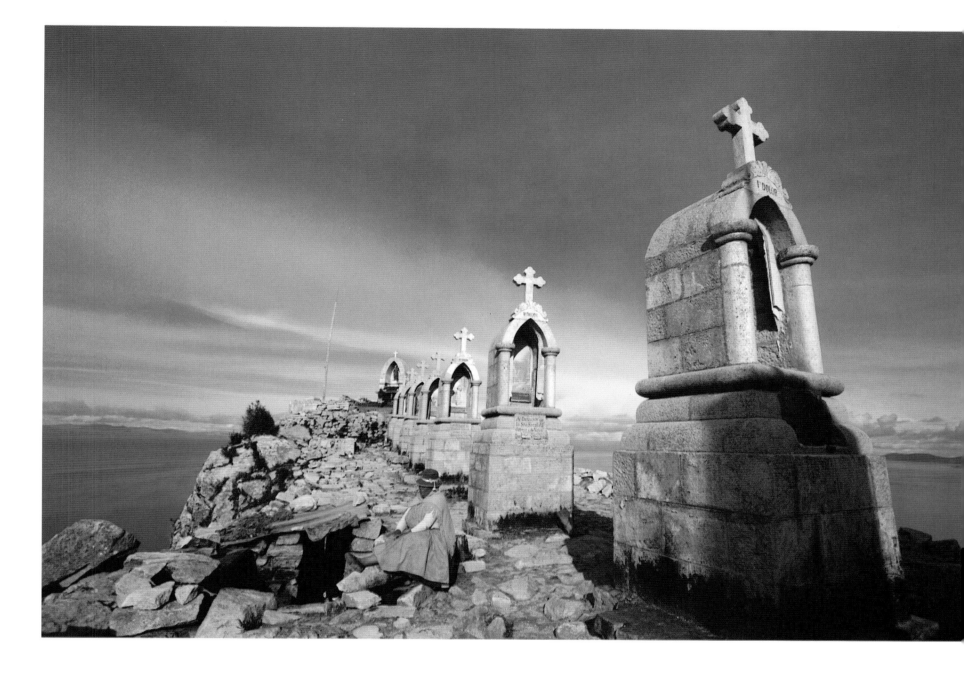

Copacabana

STATIONS OF THE CROSS

Copacabana, Bolivia, was a pilgrimage site for South American Indians long before the advent of Christianity. When the Incas invaded the area in the fifteenth century, they allowed the conquered people to maintain their deities, which were believed to reside in all the natural features of the landscape. And when Spanish Catholicism replaced the earlier forms of worship, the sacred places often remained the same. Here at Copacabana, the fourteen Stations of the Cross, which illuminate the key events of Christ's passion and death, culminate at the same summit that is still revered today by the local animistic religions.

It seemed somehow fitting that during my

Stations of the Cross,
Copacabana, Bolivia, January 1988

visit this South American Indian woman wearing North American-style clothing should be the lone guardian of the monuments of an originally European religion that are visited by pilgrims from all over the world. Perhaps the earth's sacred places can provide the meeting ground for all of us to share in life's greatest quests.

Chimborazo

MOUNTAIN OF THE ETERNAL VOYAGE

Mount Chimborazo, meaning "mountain of snow," is located in Ecuador and is the highest mountain in the Andes. Known as the King of the Cordillera, its ice-covered peak towers to a 20,571-foot (6,300 m) summit. Exploring a nearby mountain plateau, I came upon a woman and a young child working in the shelter of their domed house, which must be at one of the highest habitable altitudes on earth. They paid little attention to me as I positioned myself to photograph the complementary curves of the roof and the mountain; perhaps they felt protected by the mountain when strangers approached.

Partly due to its enormous height above the clouds, Chimborazo's snow-capped upper reaches are rarely seen. Even from this desert plateau above the tree line (opposite), the summit did its best to evade me, coyly shrouding itself in veils of cloud and revealing itself only for brief glimpses. The Quechua Indians, indigenous to the Chimborazo region, believed these mountain mists to be nekas wakani, or "true souls," which after death were transformed into clouds on their eternal journey. Seeing the phantom-like mountain emerge from the mists felt to me like another soul had achieved its ultimate destination.

Mother and child at hut,
Mount Chimborazo, Ecuador, February 1985

Alpine desert and Mount Chimborazo,
Ecuador, February 1985

St. Elias

VALLEY OF THE
GOLDEN MIST

There is a valley deep in the heart of the St. Elias Mountains that is as haunting as it is cold. Standing along the southern border between Alaska and the Yukon, these moun-tains endure winter temperatures that dip regularly to -30°F (-34°C), but the morning mists are so inviting and the light on the mountains so awe-inspiring that I forget about frozen fingers and toes. For me, this valley epitomizes one of the classic paradoxes of the Far North. The sunlight seems warm-est at the coldest hour of dawn and shines the coolest in the warmth of high noon. But the Far North has many enigmas and I am never sure during my visits if the madness I feel is

St. Elias Mountains, Haines Junction, Yukon, October 1983

the result of the biting cold, the lack of containment in this limitless space, or the outrageous splendor of the landscape.

St. Elias Mountains,
Haines Junction, Yukon, October 1983

Cathedral Rock

VORTEX OF EARTH ENERGY

Cathedral Rock is one of several outcroppings that surround the town of Sedona, Arizona. A number of these red-rock forma-tions—Bell Rock, Airport Mesa, Boynton Canyon, and Cathedral Rock—are referred to as power vortexes because of the energy fields that seem to emanate from them. For centuries, the Yavapai Indians have regarded the Sedona area as a valley of healing. Their legends speak of it as "the middle of the world" where "the Great Mother," a goddess of creation, appeared from within the earth to give birth to their nation.

Like the thousands before me who have felt drawn to Cathedral Rock, I too watched

Cathedral Rock viewed from Oak Creek,
Sedona, Arizona, September 1990

it turn a vibrant red at sunset, a time when the very rock seems to glow from within. Some claim to have had profound mystical experiences here, while others are content to merely bathe in the red glow, but even the most cynical leave with their psychic batteries charged.

It was not until I spent a night on the mesa overlooking Sedona that I experienced the unbridled energy of these high places. Time and again I watched the lightning strike the summits along the ridge in a violent clash of powerful forces above and below the earth.

Steamboat Rock in lightning storm,
Sedona, Arizona, September 1990

Mount Shasta

LOST CONTINENT OF MU

Part of the Cascade Range of dormant volcanoes, Mount Shasta rises over ten thousand feet (3,077 m), dominating the landscape near the northern border of California. Its symmetry, size, and elegance are as legendary as the mystical secrets it is reputed to harbor. Mount Shasta has the power of an enormous magnet, drawing pilgrims from around the planet. Residents of the area claim to feel a special vibrant energy here, a heightened awareness that wanes when they are away from its influence. It is also a sacred place for local native Indian groups, who use the streams flowing off the mountain for purification rituals.

One morning, seconds before the appearance of the sun, a cloud, shown opposite, drifted across the ridge, dazzling the eye with a brilliant symphony of light. With my 300 mm lens already mounted on the tripod, I had only to point and focus, exposing each frame at 1/4000 of a second. Making a series of exposures in quick succession, I once again marveled at the magic of the mountain.

Morning light on south slope,
Mount Shasta, California, November 1987

Light refraction through clouds,
Mount Shasta, California, November 1987

Each of my three visits to the region was a special event — an enchanting show of light and color: the stark beauty of morning light gracing the snow of the upper reaches, a sky of many colors, or a sunrise of ruby reds. For me, this collage of natural perfections is the mountain's greatest treasure.

Reputed to be the center of the mythical lost continent of Mu, legend speaks of Lemurians, survivors from Mu, living in caves high on Mount Shasta. Sometimes at night, it is said, their crystals can be seen flashing in the moonlight. One night the stars, as if in response to legendary rituals, shone with a brilliance I will never forget. To capture the star trails shown on the opposite page, I made a ninety-minute exposure, my tripod firmly planted on the earth as it continued its eternal spin through the heavens.

Night sky and Mount Shasta (*right*), *California, August 1988*

Predawn sky and ridge, *Mount Shasta, California, November 1987*

Devil's Marbles

EGGS OF RAINBOW SERPENT

About 250 miles (400 km) north of Alice Springs, seven square miles (18 km²) of the central Australian desert are littered with gigantic round boulders. While some of these rocks sit alone, others lie in scattered heaps, often propped against or on top of each other. One of the great Aboriginal stories handed down for thousands of years identifies these boulders as the eggs of the Rainbow Serpent, a creator being responsible for the origins of humanity and the world as the early Aborigines saw it. The serpent was also believed to be the force that transformed the flat featureless desert landscape into the world we see today.

Sunburst at Devil's Marbles,
near Tennant Creek, Australia, July 1989

Chapter Five

Places of Transformation

There are special places on this planet where events of great spiritual magnitude are reputed to have transpired. A messiah is born of virgin birth; a prophet ascends to the heavens, returning later to tell his story; the progenitors of a new empire descend from the sun on an enormous umbilical rope; a pharaoh rises from the burial chamber of a pyramid to embark on an epic voyage to the gods. These are the sites of miracles, religious occurrences, mythologically or historically significant events, places where lives and destinies have been transformed. They commemorate creation myths, places of enlightenment and momentous decisions, where religious, mythological, and temporal figures through the ages have undergone tests of courage, endured intense suffering, received new truths, or ascended into heaven. They are some of the sites most significant to the world's major religions and cultures, and all share an overwhelming magnetism that draws pilgrims from every corner of the earth.

Some events, such as Lord Buddha's enlightenment under the Bodhi Tree, or Christ's premonition of his own death while praying in the Garden of Gethsemane, are claimed by many to rest on historically documented facts, though specific details are sometimes in doubt. Other events, such as the Australian Aboriginal version of the creation of the world, are powerful mythologies that bring meaning and richness to the lives of their adherents. Unlike the world's great religious texts, many of these mythologies rely solely on an oral tradition for their continuance, but they are no less strong for not being written down. Nor, in this case, need we make distinctions among stories claimed to be based on fact and those based on myths, legends, or religious beliefs. Each is equally valid for its respective believers, a vital way of explaining their relationship to the universe.

This chapter also examines the quest for personal transformation embodied in such myths as the search for the Holy Grail or the mythical utopia, Shambhala, or Shangri-la, ideas that have provided inspiration to people across all cultures throughout human history.

During the cool July night I spent at the marbles, I felt close to the creation energies of this place. Alone in the desert with the stars overhead and the ascending moon in a deep sky, I imagined myself the first human being to arrive on the earth.

Moonrise at Devil's Marbles,
near Tennant Creek, Australia, July 1989

Sunset on Devil's Marbles,
near Tennant Creek, Australia, July 1989

Inca Creation

ISLAND OF THE SUN

In Inca legends, the creation of the universe took place on the Island of the Sun in Lake Titicaca, which straddles present-day Peru and Bolivia. Here, after a flood similar to that in the Old Testament, the creator god decreed that the sun, moon, and stars should come into being. The sun emerged from a rock on the Island of the Sun, and the shrine that commemorates the event on a barren, windswept spit of land was once venerated as the most sacred spot in the Inca Empire. The first Inca, Manco Capac, believed to be the sun god's first-born, and his wife, were molded from the fires of the sun. Climbing to earth down a huge umbilical rope, they arrived at the Island of the Sun, from whence they set out to found the mighty Inca Empire.

Arriving at Lake Titicaca, I took a rowboat across the choppy waters to the Island of the Sun. Already familiar with the creation story, I was elated to see this muted sun surrounded by feathered strands of cloud that looked as though they were being especially prepared for a re-enactment of the heroic descent.

Rope-like cloud, Island of the Sun,
Lake Titicaca, Bolivia, December 1987

Sun over Island of the Sun,
Lake Titicaca, Bolivia, December 1987

The Buddha's Cave

SYMBOL OF DARKNESS

Sometime in the last decade of the sixth century BC, Siddartha Gautama, who later became the Buddha, was born into a noble family at Lumbini in what was then India. As a young man, he renounced his family and his opulent lifestyle and left his father's palace in search of deeper truths. For six years he wandered as a hermit and a beggar, eventually settling into this cave near the village of Dungeshwari, just north of Bodhgaya.

It is not clear how long Gautama sat here in meditative fasting, but it was a time of self-denial and bitter struggle, and did not result in the achievement of the higher knowledge he was seeking. Though it would appear that the forces of darkness had triumphed, he left the cave having prepared himself for the ultimate event.

Buddha's Cave, near Dungeshwari, India, February 1989

The Bodhi Tree

HAVEN OF AWAKENING

The Bodhi Tree, or Tree of Awakening, is located in sacred gardens in the village of Bodhgaya, India. The tree that stands today is the fourth or fifth generation from the original that grew here twenty-five hundred years ago. This holiest place of Buddhism is where Gautama spent forty-nine days meditating before he attained supreme knowledge and became the Buddha, the Enlightened One.

The Bodhi Tree and ceremonial wall,
Mahabodhi Temple, Bodhgaya, India,
February 1989

Today the Mahabodhi Temple, built almost two thousand years ago, stands as the most sacred shrine to the glory of Lord Buddha. Situated at the center of the gardens with the Bodhi Tree brushing against one end, it daily receives thousands of pilgrims from around the globe. One evening during my three-day stay at Bodhgaya, I observed from the balcony of the temple a candlelight pageant around the tree. Though I found the humid heat of central India oppressive, the sanctuary of the Bodhi Tree offered a deep serenity that I have seldom experienced elsewhere.

Candlelight ceremony at the Bodhi Tree,
Mahabodhi Temple, Bodhgaya, India,
February 1989

"Nirvana"

WALKING IN THE LIGHT

The "awakening" of the Buddha under the Bodhi Tree was not only a miraculous event; it was also, more importantly, a new beginning—the seed of the great world religion of Buddhism. After leaving the gardens, Lord Buddha began his teachings, journeying to Sarnath where he met his five disciples and preached his first sermon.

When I found this solitary figure silhouetted by the golden light of a new dawn on the plains near Bodhgaya, it reminded me of the Buddha, striding out with affirmation and purpose.

Dawn light on landscape near Bodhgaya,
India, February 1989

Sarnath

MOTHER PLACE OF BUDDHISM

Silhouette of spires and doves,
Mulgandh-Kuti Vihar, Sarnath,
India, February 1989

Six miles (10 km) north of Benares in India, the ancient ruins of Sarnath mark the city where the Buddha, after reaching enlightenment, delivered his first sermon, the Dharma Chakra Pravartan. I was drawn to the Mulgandh-Kuti Vihar, an enormous temple with elaborately carved stone spires. Inside the temple are relics of the Buddha, enshrined beneath a life-sized golden statue.

In the photograph shown on the opposite page, I used the vibrant red of bougainvillea petals in the foreground to give life and warmth to the stone, and to symbolize the vitality of the Buddha's preaching, which began here and would be the catalyst to transform so many lives the world over.

**Spires of the Mulgandh-Kuti Vihar
and bougainvillea,** *Sarnath,
India, February 1989*

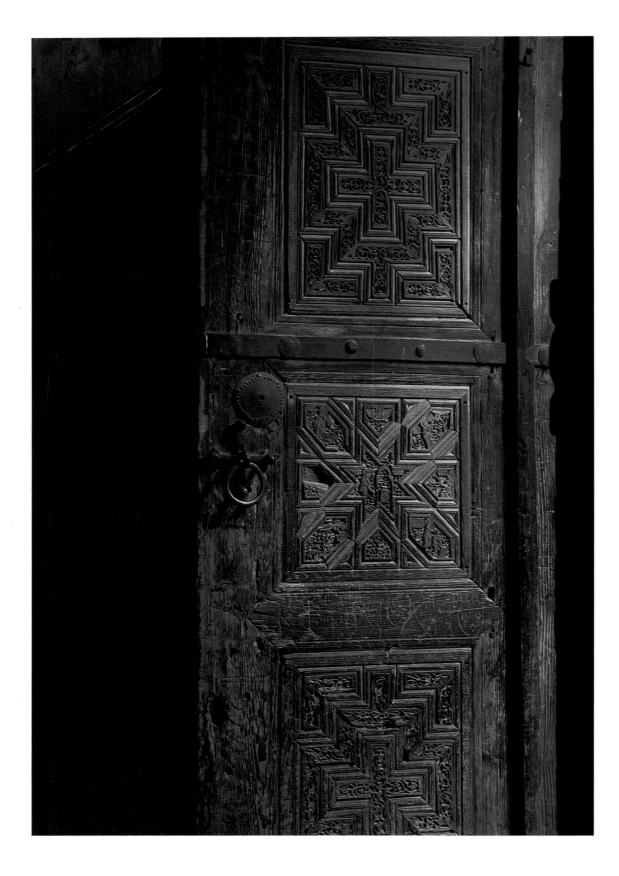

St. Catherine's

MONASTERY OF THE
BURNING BUSH

At the foot of Egypt's Mount Sinai, nestled
into the heel of the rock, is the Monastery of
St. Catherine, part of a complex of buildings
including a church, a chapel, and a mosque,
constructed in several stages from the fourth
to the sixth century. The Chapel of the
Burning Bush stands where God is believed
to have spoken to Moses out of the flames,
instructing him to go back into Egypt to
bring the Children of Israel to the Promised
Land. The monastery, built in the fourth
century AD by Helena, mother of Con-
stantine the Great, was named some centuries later for St. Catherine, a Christian living
in Alexandria who was persecuted for her
beliefs and finally beheaded in 307 AD.

This fortress-like structure has survived
the ages with remarkable strength and grace.
I was particularly attracted by the chapel's
ancient wooden door, gleaming with a
warmth that has welcomed pilgrims for
centuries.

Door, *Chapel of the Burning Bush,*
St. Catherine's Monastery, Mount Sinai,
Egypt, December 1988

Sinai

MOUNTAIN OF THE TEN
COMMANDMENTS

"And the Lord came down upon mount
Sinai, on the top of the mount: and the Lord
called Moses up to the top of the mount; and
Moses went up."

The Bible, Exodus 19:20

Retracing Moses' footsteps, I climbed the
three thousand stone steps, which begin a
short distance from St. Catherine's Monastery, to the summit of Moses' Mountain, also
known as Mount Sinai, in Egypt's Sinai
Peninsula. It was on this mountain that
Moses is reputed to have received the Ten
Commandments from the Lord and given
them, in turn, to the Children of Israel. The
gift was a set of principles to guide them in
their new lives in the Promised Land, and it
has since become a moral code for innumer-
able people around the world.

*View near summit of Moses' Mountain
(Mount Sinai), Egypt, December 1988*

"The Magi," Camel drivers and sun,
Western Desert, Egypt, December 1988

"The Magi"

STAR OF PROPHECY

"... behold, there came wise men from the east to Jerusalem, saying, where is he that is born King of the Jews? for we have seen his star in the east, and are come to worship him."

The Bible, Matthew 2:1-2

Sometimes when I photograph the bare midday sun surrounded by a darkened sky, the picture reminds me of the Bethlehem Star as I imagined it in my youth. When I found these camel drivers on a journey across the Western Desert, I immediately sought out my legendary star. The sun, in fact, is a star, crucial to the evolution of life on earth, though some astronomers believe the star that guided the Magi to Bethlehem was more likely an extremely brilliant comet.

"Nativity," Camel drivers dismantling at sunset, Giza, Egypt, December 1988

"Nativity"

BIRTH OF A MESSIAH

". . . and, lo, the star, which they saw in the east, went before them, till it came and stood over where the young child was. . . . And when they were come into the house, they saw the young child with Mary his mother, and fell down, and worshipped him: and when they had opened their treasures, they presented unto him gifts: gold, and frankincense, and myrrh."

The Bible, Matthew 2:9-11

The evening of the same day I photographed the "Magi" on the opposite page, the sun seemed to stop in its descent from the heavens, capturing a timeless image and encompassing what must have been very like the figures of the Nativity within its glowing orb. Though scholars dispute the actual date, the story of Jesus' birth has had such impact on mankind that virtually every culture dates its present-day calendar from the year of this event. The scene shown here, photographed near the Great Pyramid in Egypt, symbolizes for me the miracle of Christ's birth. The actual Church of the Nativity in Bethlehem, Israel, is one of the most holy places of pilgrimage for Christians worldwide.

Galilee

SEA OF CHRIST'S MIRACLES

The Sea of Galilee, located in Israel's Jordan Valley, is a large inland lake rimmed by many holy sites from the New Testament: Capernaum, Tiberius, Tabgha, Migdal, and the Mount of Beatitudes—places where Christ is said to have performed miracles and healed the sick. Galilee is perhaps best known, however, as the stormy sea where Christ walked upon the waters and encouraged his disciple Peter to do the same. But Peter was afraid and began to sink, "And immediately Jesus stretched forth his hand, and caught him, and said unto him, O thou of little faith, wherefore didst thou doubt?" *(The Bible, Matthew 14:30–31)*

The evening that I photographed the Sea of Galilee it was calm and the setting sun traced a golden path upon the waters, as though revealing the place where Christ had walked.

Reflection of sunset,
Sea of Galilee, Israel, January 1989

Mount of Olives

HILLSIDE OF MEDITATION

Skyline of the Old City from Mount of Olives, Jerusalem, Israel, January 1989

The Mount of Olives is a height of land on the eastern outskirts of the Old City of Jerusalem in Israel; it is named for the groves of olive trees that grace its slopes. Because of its association with Christ's final hours on earth, the hillside has become synonymous with his mission work, although very little, if any, of it actually occurred there. It did serve, however, as a retreat where he went to meditate. Traditionally, it was the place where Christ wept over Jerusalem before entering the gates of the city on Palm Sunday.

Some of the present-day hillside is preserved as a natural haven from which I could see the walls of the Old City of Jerusalem. By focusing on the foreground grasses, thus obscuring the shapes of Jerusalem's modern skyline, I was able to re-create the city as Jesus might have seen it in the golden evening light nearly two thousand years ago.

Gethsemane

GARDEN OF AGONY

The Garden of Gethsemane is on the lower slopes of the Mount of Olives within sight of the ancient walls of Jerusalem in Israel. Though Christ had come here to pray many times, the garden is most closely associated with the anguish of his final hours. Here, after the Last Supper, Jesus came and wept, knowing that in a short time his disciple Judas would betray him to the Roman soldiers, thus beginning the inexorable chain of events that would lead to his death on the Cross.

In order to reflect the somber tone of this awe-inspiring historic event, I waited for a rainy day to photograph in the garden. When I found this single green leaf contrasted with the darkness of the olive tree, I saw in it a symbol of the living Christ standing alone against the cruel forces of the world.

Detail of bark, olive tree, *dieffenbachia leaf in foreground, Garden of Gethsemane, Jerusalem, Israel, January 1989*

The Garden Tomb

CAVE OF THE
CRUCIFIED CHRIST

"Now in the place where he was crucified
there was a garden."

The Bible, John 19:41

Following Jesus' crucifixion on a hill called Golgotha just outside the old walls of Jerusalem, Joseph of Arimathea wrapped the body in a clean linen cloth and moved it to a nearby sepulchre. Discovered and excavated in 1882, the tomb shown here dates back to the Roman period, and both it and its surroundings reflect fairly accurately the description of Christ's tomb in the Bible. Nearby, the Church of the Holy Sepulchre also claims to mark the spot where Jesus was buried. Both are revered spots of Christian pilgrimage, but while the church has a multitude of shrines illustrating significant events in Christ's last days on earth, the Garden Tomb is a simple, quiet haven where Christians from around the world come to worship.

Tomb of Christ, Garden Tomb,
Jerusalem, Israel, January 1989

Earthen Cave

SYMBOL OF THE EMPTY TOMB

When I visited the sanctuary of the Garden Tomb, the sun burst through the clouds and shone into a small enclosure in the side of an earthen wall, as if alerting me to a place previously overlooked. I felt drawn to the special glow of the cavern shown here, even though I knew the designated tomb of Christ's burial was situated a short distance away. Finding the exact place so much in dispute did not seem to matter. Simply being there was to experience the abiding peace that permeates this garden where Christ is believed to have risen from the dead.

Sunlight on cave wall,
near Jerusalem, Israel, December 1988

Dome of the Rock

ANCIENT MOSQUE OF ISLAM

To Moslems, one of the holiest places of Islam is the Dome of the Rock mosque in Jerusalem. When I photographed the topmost roof ornament on the dome, shown here, the sun broke free of its bondage in the clouds, and it was as if Allah, God of Islam, had revealed His presence and bestowed a blessing upon this ancient holy place. It reminded me of a passage from the Koran:

"By the sun and its growing brightness, And by the moon when it follows it, And by the day when it reveals its glory, And by the night when it draws a veil over it, And by the heaven and its making, And by the earth and its spreading out, And by the soul and its perfection, And He revealed to it what is wrong for it and what is right for it. He indeed truly prospers who purifies it."

The Koran, Surah 91:1–10

Sun and roof piece, *Dome of the Rock mosque, Jerusalem, Israel, December 1988*

The Dome of the Rock is an exquisite mosque in the holy city of Jerusalem, built at the summit of the ancient Mount Moriah, a site extremely sacred to the Islamic faith and to Judaism, and also of historical interest to Christians. In the tenth century BC, King Solomon is reputed to have built the first temple on this spot, believed by many to be the site of the legendary altar where, according to the Bible, Abraham prepared to sacrifice his son Isaac around 2000 BC. The present structure, the most recent of several temples that succeeded Solomon's, and Jerusalem's most prominent landmark today, was completed around 691 AD. A major center for Islamic worship, it is also open to pilgrims of all faiths, who, like the Moslems, remove their shoes at the door in a gesture of respect for the deity.

Exterior, *Dome of the Rock mosque, Jerusalem, Israel, December 1988*

"In the name of Allah, the Gracious, the Merciful. Glory be to Him who made His servant go by night from the Sacred Temple to the Furthest Temple whose surroundings We have blessed, that We might show him some of Our signs. He alone hears all and observes all."

The Koran, Surah 17:1–2

The Dome of the Rock is built directly over an exposed rocky outcropping of the legendary Mount Moriah. This spot has special significance for Moslems as the point of departure for Mohammed's "night journey." Traditionally, it was from this rock that Mohammed, founder of Islam, ascended from earth for a journey through the seven heavens to speak with the great prophets and to commune with Allah. On this journey, Mohammed is believed to have received from Allah the words of the Koran, as well as many other truths, some too sacred even to be recorded in the holy texts.

Place of the night journey,
Dome of the Rock mosque, Jerusalem, Israel, December 1988

The Great Pyramid

MONUMENT OF MYSTERY

The Great Pyramid, the largest man-made structure of its kind on earth, stands on the Giza Plateau ten miles (16 km) west of Cairo in Egypt. Begun during the period of the Fourth Dynasty, 2613-2494 BC, the pyramid is attributed to the pharaoh Cheops, but experts have been unable to discover if he was actually entombed there, or if, indeed, the pyramid ever contained anything. Arab explorers in the ninth century AD, the first to gain entrance to the pyramid as far as anyone knows, reported the tomb to be entirely empty of both mummy and treasure. Though numerous interpretations have been offered by scholars down through the ages, no one thus far has successfully explained any of the mysteries associated with this enigmatic structure. Whatever may have been the original intentions of its builders, the Great Pyramid stands today as living testimony to man's endless quest for the eternal. Known to the ancient Egyptians as Ta Khut, or The Light, the Great Pyramid touches the mystic within us all.

The Great Pyramid,
Giza, Egypt, December 1988

The King's Chamber

PREPARATION FOR
THE UNDERWORLD

The King's Chamber, deep within the pyramid of Cheops, was where the mummy of the pharaoh should have been entombed to begin his spiritual journey to the nether world. Here, according to ancient tradition, lavish treasures, the finest foods, wines, servants and pets, and barques for his heavenly voyage would have been sealed into special storage areas. But nothing of this nature has ever been found.

In a meditation prior to entering the King's Chamber, I envisaged twelve candles surrounding the empty sarcophagus and accordingly, I took them with me and lit them as an offering to Amun, the sun god, whose spirit, I felt, still watches over this ancient holy place. In order to depict the sun god's abiding presence, I made a double exposure, photographing the candle-lit crypt and combining it with my image of the sun setting over the Western Desert.

"Pharaoh's Journey," *Composite of sun and sarcophagus, King's Chamber, Great Pyramid, Giza, Egypt, December 1988*

Glastonbury

GATEWAY TO THE CELTIC OTHER WORLD

Overlooking the ancient town of Glastonbury in southern England, Glastonbury Tor is an oblong hill encircled by a mysterious serpentine footpath, and is a modern-day place of pilgrimage for people of many faiths and persuasions. The spiral path is believed to have some connection to the old Great Goddess cult, which would date religious activity on the site to some point beyond 5000 BC. Crowning the Tor is St. Michael's Tower, all that remains of a church built on the site during the fourteenth century.

Churches were commonly built on sites of former pagan worship, both to provide some continuity in the spiritual lives of the surrounding community, and also to Christianize the site by driving out the old pagan spirits.

Like the Great Pyramid in Egypt, the Glastonbury Tor has been recognized as a powerful focal point of earth energies. One cannot help but feel, as I did in the King's Chamber, on Mount Shasta, and at the Bodhi Tree, that there are special places on the earth where the veil between our world and the other world is as thin as it is elusive. Looking at St. Michael's Tower through a 3000 mm lens (view shown opposite), I indeed felt as though I were gazing through the cosmos at another world.

South slope of the Tor and St. Michael's Tower,
Glastonbury, England, August 1989

Silhouette of St. Michael's Tower and sun,
Glastonbury, England, August 1989

Chalice Well

QUEST FOR THE HOLY GRAIL

The Chalice Well Garden lies at the foot of the Glastonbury Tor and is believed by some to harbor the cup from which Christ drank at the Last Supper. Even before the Christian era, the perpetual waters from this well, known also as Blood Spring, were revered for what was believed to be their magical life-giving power. Tradition has it that Joseph of Arimathea, who wrapped Christ's body in its shroud and took it to the Garden Tomb, received the chalice after the Last Supper and brought it to Glastonbury. In the Arthurian legends, the knights of the Round Table sought this Holy Grail, believing that only those of pure heart would be led to its resting place.

My quest began when I came upon a list of the world's twelve most sacred places, introduced by a modern-day mystic named Robert Coon. When I arrived in Glastonbury after circling the globe, it was Robert who gave me this goblet to photograph at the Chalice Well.

Goblet and waterfall, *Chalice Well Gardens, Glastonbury, England, August 1989*

Ise Shrine

HOLY WATERS OF THE KAMI

If the Chalice Well is reputed to have the holiest waters in Christendom, Ise, on the east coast of Japan, marks the place of most sacred waters in Shinto belief. The bamboo cups in this photograph are dipped into the sacred well and with a sip of the holy waters, pilgrims (more than six million annually) receive the abundance of life from the kami, deities that express themselves in the works of nature. Just as it is said that only the pure of heart may find the Holy Grail, so in Shinto belief one must be ritually purified before approaching the kami.

Shinto shrines are always found amid the beauties of nature because the kami are embodied in all its manifestations. I felt completely at home here in Ise, immersing myself in the serenity of the natural world, which is the kami way.

Bamboo cups at the sacred well,
Naiku Shrine, Ise, Japan, April 1989

Jingu

THE GRAND SHRINE OF ISE

In addition to its sacred waters, the Jingu shrines at Ise, Japan, have been known since medieval times as the holiest of all Shinto sanctuaries, although the two main shrines were established much earlier than that—Naiku in 4 BC, and Geku in 478 AD. Japanese mythology points to Amaterasu, the sun goddess, as ancestress of the Imperial dynasty and guardian of the Japanese nation. Though accessible for many centuries to only royalty and priests, the shrines were eventually opened to the masses, who often without warning would respond to a divine call and arrive in multitudes to pay homage to the powers that created their nation. In 1705 it was reported that three and a half million pilgrims converged on Ise in a one-month period. Like my experience at the Taj Mahal, however, I found that Ise could easily accommodate the thousands who visit daily and still maintain the quiescence of its sylvan glades.

Isuzu River at Naiku Grand Shrine,
Ise, Japan, April 1989

It is believed that originally the untouched forest at Ise was the place of worship. Nowadays, about thirty wooden buildings are scattered among the trees, and since the seventh century, the shrines have been ritually rebuilt and rededicated every twenty years, a symbolic expression of gratitude to the sun goddess for the bounty of her blessings.

In front of the Naiku Grand Shrine is the Uji Bridge, shown here, flanked by two torii, or sacred gates. The bridge spans the sacred Isuzu River, where worshippers since ancient times have purified themselves before making their way to the holy shrine.

To those of the Shinto faith who visit the site, Ise maintains its singular importance as the earthly home of Amaterasu, sun goddess and founder of the nation. When the rains abate and the clouds of mist evaporate, she can be seen keeping watch from above, though even in the midst of the warm soothing rains of Japan, one is aware of her abiding presence.

Uji Bridge at Naiku Grand Shrine, Ise, Japan, April 1989

Shambhala

THE SACRED PLACE
OF OUR DREAMS

When I was young, I used to take a fishing pole to the banks of the Saskatchewan River, a short distance from my home. I never managed to catch much, but that did not stop me from trying. I would stand at the river's edge and imagine the exotic life that lurked just beyond my grasp. I was reminded of my dreams as I watched some wide-eyed Japanese children seeing the sacred Isuzu River at Ise for the first time. They gazed intently into the translucent waters where carp emerged to feed, perhaps wondering which fish were the kami, or where exactly the sun goddess languished in the afternoons.

These same nostalgic feelings came over me when I found this Hawaiian boy fishing off a rocky point on the north shore of the Big Island. It was a weekday, so he was probably playing hooky from school, but his yen for adventure, the need to follow his dreams, and his quest for the big one will be as crucial to him as all his schooling combined.

Boy fishing, *north shore,*
Big Island, Hawaii, February 1987

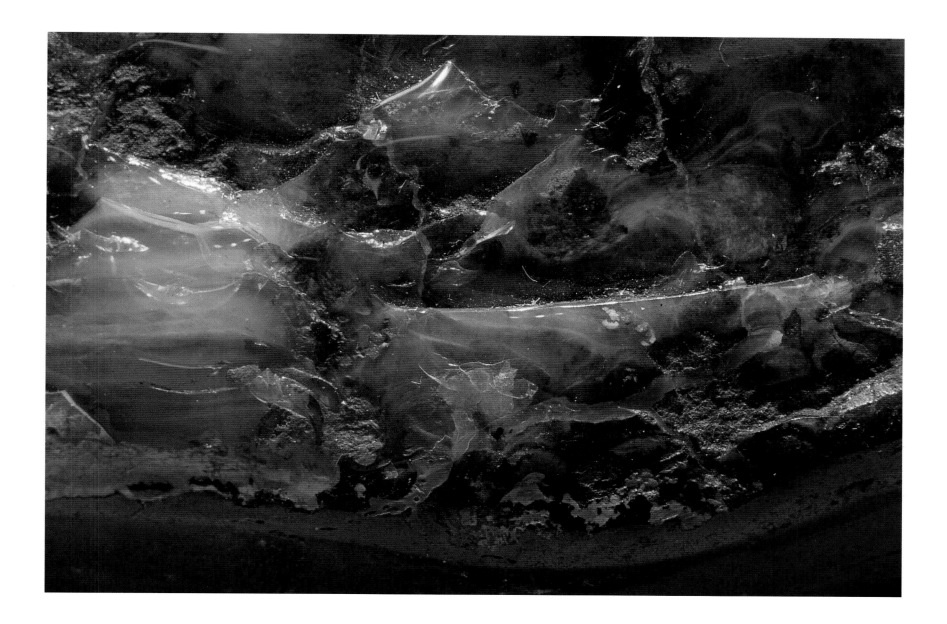

Shambhala is a mythical utopia believed to lie somewhere beyond the Himalayas, perhaps in Tibet or Mongolia. It is the lost city of our dreams, an ideal land where peace endures, a secret paradise where man lives in perfect harmony with his fellow man and his surroundings. It is the magical kingdom of childhood, often lost and yearned for in our adult years, yet rarely regained. But it is always there, just beyond the horizon.

Virtually every culture and religion has its stories of Shambhala. But the journey to the lost city is not physical; it is a voyage of personal discovery. And because the source is ultimately within ourselves, the possibility of finding Shambhala exists for us all.

"Shambhala," detail of opal rock, *Brisbane, Australia, August 1989*

References

Acosta-Solis, M. et al. *Ecuador in the Shadow of the Volcanoes*. Quito: Ediciones Libri Mundi, 1981.

The Age of God Kings: Time Frame 3000–1500 B.C. Alexandria, VA: Time Life, 1987.

Allen, D. *Totem Poles of the Northwest*. Surrey, BC: Hancock House Publishers, 1977.

Allen, Paula Gunn. *The Sacred Hoop: Recovering the Feminine in American Indian Traditions*. Boston: Beacon Press, 1986.

Alonzo, Gualberto Zapata. *An Overview of the Mayan World*. Merida, Mexico: n.p., 1987.

Alpers, Antony. [illus.: Patrick Hanly]. *Maori Myths and Tribal Legends*. Auckland, New Zealand: Longman Paul Ltd., 1964.

Argüelles, José. *The Mayan Factor: The Path Beyond Technology*. Sante Fe, NM: Bear and Co., 1987.

Ashby, Gene. *A Guide to Pohnpei*. Eugene, OR: Rainy Day Press, 1983, 1987.

Ashwell, Reg. *Indian Tribes of the Northwest*. Surrey, BC: Hancock House Publishers, 1977.

Australia Insight Guide. Hong Kong: APA Publications, 1987.

Bacon, Ron. [illus.: Robert Jahnke]. *Maori Legends: The Creation Stories*. Auckland, New Zealand: Beckett Sterling Ltd., 1985.

Bailby, Edouard. *The Keys to Equador*. Bréa Editions, 1983.

Barbarian Tides: Time Frame 1500–600 B.C. Alexandria, VA: Time Life, 1987.

Barber, Robin. *Greece*. Blue Guide. London: A and C Black, 1988.

Barnett, Stephen. *Magnificent New Zealand*. Auckland, New Zealand: William Collins Publishers Ltd., 1982.

Baumgartner, Anne S. *A Comprehensive Dictionary of the Gods from Abaasy to Zvoruna*. Carve Communications, 1984.

Beckwith, Martha. *Hawaiian Mythology*. Honolulu: University of Hawaii Press, 1970.

Bendure, Glenda, and Ned Friary. *Micronesia: A Travel Survival Kit*. Victoria, Australia: Lonely Planet Publications, 1988.

Benzinger, Charles. *Chaco Journey: Remembrance and Awakening*. Santa Fe, NM: Timewindow Publications, 1988.

Berlitz, Charles. *Atlantis: The 8th Continent*. New York: Fawcett Crest Ballantine Books, 1984.

Bernbaum, Edwin. *The Way to Shambhala*. New York: Anchor Press/Doubleday, 1980.

———. *Sacred Mountains of the World*. San Francisco: Sierra Club, 1990.

Best, Elsdon. *Maori Religion and Mythology*. Part I. 1924. Reprint. Wellington, New Zealand, 1976.

———. *Forestlore of the Maori*. Wellington, New Zealand: E.C. Keating Government Printer, 1977.

———. *The Astronomical Knowledge of the Maori*. Wellington, New Zealand: VR Ward Government Printer, 1986.

Bisignani, J.D. *Hawaii Handbook*. Chico, CA: Moon Publications, 1987.

Black, Star et al. *Bali Insight Guide*. Hong Kong: APA Publications, 1987.

Bloomgarden, Richard. *The Easy Guide to Palenque*. Mexico DF: Editur, SA, 1988.

Boardman, Peter. *Sacred Summits*. London: Arrow Books, 1982.

Bonavia, Judy. *The Yangtze River*. Hong Kong: China Guide Series, 1985.

Bord, Janet and Colin. *Mysterious Britain: Ancient Secrets of the United Kingdom and Ireland*. London: Paladin, 1974.

———. *Sacred Waters: Holy Wells and Water Lore in Britain and Ireland*. Great Britain: Paladin/Collins, 1986.

Breeden, Stanley, and Belinda Wright. *Kakadu: Looking After the Country—The Gagudju Way*. Brookvale, Australia: Simon and Schuster, 1989.

Browning, Iain. *Petra*. rev.ed. London: Chatto and Windus, 1982.

Brunton, Paul. *A Search in Secret India*. ME: Kenneth Thurston Hurst, 1985.

Burger, Julian. *The Gaia Atlas of First Peoples: A Future for the Indigenous World*. New York: Anchor Books/Doubleday, 1990.

Burl, Aubrey. *Prehistoric Astronomy and Ritual*. Aylesbury, England: Shire Publications, 1983.

Caduto, Michael J., and Joseph Bruchac. *Keepers of the Earth: Native Stories and Environmental Activities for Children*. Saskatoon: Fifth House Publishers, 1989.

Caldwell, Joseph R., and Robert Hall, eds. *Hopewellian Studies*. Scientific Papers, Vol. XII. Illinois State Museum, Springfield, IL, 1977.

Campbell, Joseph. *The Inner Reaches of Outer Space: Metaphor as Myth and as Religion*. New York: Harper and Row, 1986.

———. *The Mythic Image*. Princeton: Princeton University Press, 1974.

Carter, Anthony. *This is Haida*. Vancouver: Agency Press Ltd., 1968.

Carver, Norman F. Jr. *Silent Cities of Mexico and the Maya*. Kalamazoo, MI: Documan Press Ltd., 1986.

Chatwin, Bruce. *The Songlines*. New York: Penguin, 1988.

Chester, Carol. *The Hawaiian Islands*. New York: Hippocrene Books, 1987.

Chetwynd, Tom. *Dictionary of Sacred Myth*. Unwin Paperbacks, 1986.

Childress, David Hatcher. *Lost Cities and Ancient Mysteries of South America*. Stelle, IL: Adventures Unlimited Press, 1986.

———. *Lost Cities of China, Central Asia and India*. Stelle, IL: Adventures Unlimited Press, 1987.

Churchward, Col. James. *The Lost Continent of Mu*. NM: BE Books, 1987.

Coe, Michael D. *The Maya*. 4th ed. London: Thames and Hudson, 1987.

Corbett, Cynthia. *Power Trips: Journeys to Sacred Sites as a Way of Transformation*. Sante Fe, NM: Timewindow Publications, 1988.

Cotta Vaz, Mark. *Spirit in the Land*. New York: Signet Paperback, 1988.

Cox, J. Halley, and Edward Stasek. *Hawaiian Petroglyphs*. Honolulu: Bishop Museum Press, 1970.

Creation magazine, May/June 1985 and Sept/Oct 1987.

Critchlow, Keith. *Time Stands Still*. New York: St. Martin's Press, 1982.

Dalai Lama, His Holiness the, and Galen Rowell. *My Tibet*. Berkeley: University of California Press, 1990.

Dragoo, Don W. *Mounds for the Dead*. Pittsburg, PA: Carnegie Museum of Natural History, 1963.

Dube, D. N., and Shalini Saran. *Taj Mahal*. New Delhi: Roli Books International, 1985.

Earhart, H. Byron. *Religions of Japan*. San Francisco: Harper and Row, 1984.

Eliot, Sir Charles. *Hinduism and Buddhism*. Vols. 1, 2, 3. New Delhi: Sri Satguru Publications, 1921, 1988.

Ellwood, Robert S., and Richard Pilgrim. *Japanese Religion*. Englewood Cliffs, NJ: Prentice-Hall Inc., 1985.

Emerson, Nathaniel B. *Pele and Hiiaka: A Myth from Hawaii*. Rutland, VT: Charles E. Tuttle Co., 1978.

Empires Ascendant: Time Frame 400 B.C.–200 A.D. Alexandria, VA: Time Life, 1987.

Erdoes, Richard, and Alfonson Ortiz, eds. *American Indian Myths and Legends*. New York: Pantheon Books, 1984.

Feats and Wisdom of the Ancients. Alexandria, VA: Time Life, 1990.

Fell, Barry. *America B.C.* New York: Pocket Books, Simon and Schuster, 1976, 1989.

Ferguson, Ron. *Chasing the Wild Goose: The Iona Community*. Collins, Fount Paperbacks, 1988.

Fidler, J. Havelock. *Earth Energy: A Dowser's Investigation of Ley Lines*. Wellingborough, England: Aquarian Press, 1983, 1988.

Fire of Life: The Smithsonian Book of the Sun. Washington, DC: Smithsonian Exposition Books, 1981.

Fisher, Robert, ed. *Crown Insider's Guide: Mexico 1987/88*. New York: Crown Books, 1987.

Fix, Wm. *Pyramid Odyssey*. Urbanna, VA: Mercury Media, 1978, 1984.

Fodor's 89 Guide to Mexico. New York: Fodor Travel Publications, 1988.

Fodor's 90 Guide to Cancun, Cozumel and Yucatan Peninsula. New York: Fodor Travel Publications, 1989.

Folberg, Niel. *In a Desert Land*. New York: Abbeville Press, 1987.

Fortune, Dion. *Glastonbury: Avalon of the Heart*. rev. ed. Wellingborough, England: Aquarian Press, 1986.

Foster, Lynn V. and Lawrence. *Fielding's Mexico 1988*. New York: Fielding Travel Books, Morrow and Co. Inc., 1988.

Fox, Matthew. *The Coming of the Cosmic Christ*. San Francisco: Harper and Row, 1988.

Frazier, Charles. *Adventuring in the Andes*. San Francisco: Sierra Club Books, 1985.

Frick, Thomas, ed. *Sacred Theory of the Earth*. Berkeley, CA: North Atlantic Books, 1986.

Frommer's Hawaii 1989–90. New York: Simon and Schuster, 1989.

Frost, Peter. *Exploring Cuzco*. Lima, Peru: Bradt Enterprises, 1984.

Gallenkamp, Charles. *Maya: The Riddle and Rediscovery of a Lost Civilization*. 3rd rev. ed. New York: Viking, 1985.

George, Chief Dan. *My Spirit Soars*. Surrey, BC: Hancock House Publishers, 1982.

Gnass, Jeff. *Hawaii: Magnificent Wilderness*. Englewood, CO: Westcliffe Publishers, Inc.

Golia, Jack de. *Everglades: The Story Behind the Scenery*. Las Vegas: KC Publications, 1978.

Hadingham, Evan. *Lines to the Mountain Gods: Nazca and the Mysteries of Peru*. New York: Random House, 1987.

Halpin, Marjorie M. *Totem Poles: An Illustrated Guide*. Vancouver: University of British Columbia Press, 1981.

Hamilton, Edith. *Mythology: Timeless Tales of Gods and Heroes*. Meridian, 1940, 1969.

Hamilton, Virgina, and Barry Moses. *In the Beginning*. Orlando, FL: Harcourt Brace Jovanovich, 1988.

Harpur, James, and Jennifer Westwood. *The Atlas of Legendary Places*. New York: Weidenfeld and Nicolson, 1989.

Heinberg, Richard. *Memories and Visions of Paradise: Exploring the Universal Myth of a Lost Golden Age*. Los Angeles, CA: Jeremy Tarcher, 1989.

Hemming, John, and Edward Ranney. *Monuments of the Incas*. Boston: Little, Brown and Company, 1982.

Howard-Gordon, Frances. *Glastonbury: Maker of Myths*. Glastonbury, England: Gothic Image, 1982.

Hyams, Edward. *A History of Gardens and Gardening*. New York: Praeger, 1971.

Indonesia Guide. Jakarta: American Express Co., n.d.

Jackson, Bernard. *Places of Pilgrimage*. London: Geoffrey Chapman, 1989.

Jarow, Rick. *In Search of the Sacred: a pilgrimage to holy places*. Wheaton, IL: Theosophical Publishing House, 1986.

Jarver, Peter. *Kakadu Country*. Darwin, Australia: Thunderhead Photographics, 1986.

———. *The Top End of Down Under*. Darwin, Australia: Thunderhead Publishing, 1988.

Jilek, Wolfgang. *Indian Healing: Shamanic Ceremonialism in the Pacific Northwest Today*. Surrey, BC: Hancock House Publishers, 1982.

Johnson, Russell, and Kerry Moran. *The Sacred Mountain of Tibet: On Pilgrimage to Kailas*. Rochester, VT: Park St. Press, 1989.

Jordan. Amman, Jordan: Jordan Distribution Agency, 1986.

Kaplan, Fredric. *China 1989 Guidebook*. Teaneck, NJ: Eurasia Press, 1989.

Kelemen, Pal. *Art of the Americas: Ancient and Hispanic*. New York: Thomas Crowell, 1969.

Keswick, Maggie. *Chinese Garden*. Great Britain: Academy Editions, 1978.

Kew, Della, and P.E. Goddard. *Indian Art and Culture of the Northwest Coast*. Surrey, BC: Hancock House Publishers, 1974.

Khalsa, Parmatma Singh, ed. *A Pilgrim's Guide to Planet Earth*. CA: Spiritual Community Publications, 1981.

Khanna, Madhu. *Yantra: The Tantric Symbol of Cosmic Unity*. London: Thames and Hudson, 1979.

Kindred Spirit magazine. Autumn 1989.

Krupp, Dr. E.C. *Echoes of the Ancient Skies: Astronomy of Lost Civilizations*. New York: Harper and Row, 1983.

Lamoureux, Charles H. *Trailside Plants of Hawaii's National Parks*. Honolulu: Hawaii Natural History Assoc., 1976.

Lampo, Hubert, and Paul Pieter Koster. *Arthur and the Grail*. London: Sidgewick and Jackson, 1988.

Lawlor, Robert. *Sacred Geometry: Philosophy and Practice*. London: Thames and Hudson, 1987.

Layton, Robert. *Uluru: An Aboriginal History of Ayers' Rock*. Australia: University of Aboriginal Studies, 1986.

Lehrman, Fredric. *The Sacred Landscape*. Berkeley, CA: Celestial Arts Publishing, 1988.

Leonard, George. *The Silent Pulse*. New York: E.P. Dutton, 1986.

Lewin, Roger. *Darwin's Forgotten World*. Los Angeles, CA: Reed Books, Bison Books Ltd., 1978.

Lings, Martin. *Ancient Belief and Modern Superstitions*. Boston: Unwin Paperbacks, Mandala Books, 1980.

Lonegren, Sid. *Spiritual Dowsing*. Glastonbury, England: Gothic Image Publications, 1986.

Lopez, Barry. *Arctic Dreams: Imagination and Desire in a Northern Landscape*. New York: Charles Scribner's Sons, 1986.

———. *Crossing Open Ground*. London, England: Pan Books, 1989.

McClellan, Catharine. *Part of the Land, Part of the Water: A History of the Yukon Indians*. Vancouver: Douglas and McIntyre, 1987.

MacDonald, George F. *Ninstints: Haida World Heritage Site*. Vancouver: University of British Columbia Press, 1983.

MacDonald, Gordon A., and Douglas H. Hubbard. *Volcanoes of the National Parks in Hawaii*. rev. by Richard W. Hazlett. Honolulu: Hawaii Natural History Association, 1982.

McGhee, Robert. *Ancient Canada*. Ottawa: Canadian Museum of Civilization, 1989.

Mackichan, David. *The Pilgrim's Way to Iona*. Craignure, Isle of Mull: 1987.

Maclagan, David. *Creation Myths: Man's Introduction to the World*. London: Thames and Hudson, 1977.

MacNab, Peter. *Mull and Iona: Highways and Byways*. Barr, Scotland: Luath Press Ltd., 1988.

McNaughton, Trudie, comp. *Countless Signs: The New Zealand landscape in literature*. Auckland, New Zealand: Reed Methuen Publishers Ltd., 1986.

McQueen, Ian. *Japan: A Travel Survival Kit*. Victoria, Australia: Lonely Planet Series, 1981.

Maldonado-Robles, Luis, and Christian Sarramon. *Galapagos Pacific*. Paris: Editions D.S., 1982.

Mann, Nicholas R. *Sedona—Sacred Earth: A Guide to Geomantic Applications in the Red Rock Country*. Prescott, AZ: Zivah, 1989.

The March of Islam: Time Frame 600–800 A.D. Alexandria, VA: Time Life, 1988.

Marzuki, Yazir, and Toeti Herati. *Borobudur*. Indonesia: Djambatan, 1982, 1985, 1987.

Matlock, Gary, and Warren Scott. *Enemy Ancestors—The Anasazi World with a Guide to Sites*. Northland Press, 1988.

Matsunami, Kodo. *Introducing Buddhism*. Tokyo: Charles E. Tuttle, 1976.

Maud, Ralph. *A Guide to B.C. Indian Myth and Legend*. Vancouver: Talon Books, 1982.

May, John. *The Greenpeace Book of Antarctica*. Toronto: MacMillan, 1988.

Melville, J. McKim, and Claudia Putnam. *Prehistoric Astronomy in the Southwest*. Boulder, CO: Johnson Books, 1989.

Mendelssohn, Kurt. *The Riddle of the Pyramids*. London: Thames and Hudson, 1986.

Merz, Blanche. *Points of Cosmic Energy*. Essex, England: C.W. Daniel Co. Ltd., 1987.

Michell, John. *The Earth Spirit: Its Ways, Shrines and Mysteries*. London: Thames and Hudson, 1975.

———. *Secrets of the Stones: The Story of Astro-Archeology*. New York: Penguin, 1977.

———. *The Traveller's Key to Sacred England*. London: Harrap Columbus, 1989.

Miles, Greg. *Wildlife of Kakadu*. n.p., n.d.

Moerdowo, Dr. R. *Ceremonies in Bali*. Bhratau, Jakarta, 1973.

Moore, Tui De Roy. *Galapagos: Islands Lost in Time*. New York: Viking Press, 1980.

Morford, Mark, and Robert Lenardon. *Classical Mythology*. New York: Longman, 1971, 1977, 1985.

Morris, Walter F., and Jeffrey J. Foxx. *Living Maya*. New York: Harry N. Abrams, 1987.

Morrison, Tony. *The Andes*. Amsterdam: Time Life, 1975.

Morrow, Patrick. *Beyond Everest: Quest for the Seven Summits*. Camden East, ON: Camden House Publishing Ltd., 1986.

Muir, Richard. *Traveller's History of Britain and Ireland*. London: Mermaid Books, 1987.

Mullikan, Mary Augusta, and Anna M. Hotchkis. *The Nine Sacred Mountains of China*. Hong Kong: Vetch and Lee, 1973.

Mungall, Constance, and Digby McLaren, eds. *Planet Under Stress*. Don Mills, ON: Oxford University Press, 1990.

Munro, Eleanor. *On Glory Roads: A Pilgrim's Book about Pilgrimage*. New York: Thames and Hudson, 1988.

Myers, Dr. Norman, ed. *Gaia: an atlas of planet management*. New York: Anchor Books, Doubleday and Co. Ltd., 1984.

Mystic Places. Alexandria, VA: Time Life, 1987.

Natural Wonders of the World. Montreal: The Reader's Digest Association Inc., 1980.

Neidjie, Bill. *Australia's Kakadu Man*. Darwin, Australia: Resource Manager's Pty. Ltd., 1985.

Oey, Eric, ed. *Indonesia Insight Guide*. Singapore: APA Publications, 1988.

Ono, Sokyo. *Shinto: The Kami Way*. Rutland, VT: Charles E. Tuttle, 1962.

Orbell, Margaret. *Hawaii: A New Approach to Maori Tradition*. Christchurch, New Zealand: University of Canterbury, 1985.

Orbell, Margaret, and Geoff Moon. *The Natural World of the Maori*. Auckland, New Zealand: Collins, 1985.

Ortiz, Alfonso, ed. *Handbook of North American Indians*. Vol. 9, *Southwest*. Washington, DC: Smithsonian Institute, 1979.

Pathy, T.V. *Ajanta, Ellora, and Aurangabad Caves, an appreciation*. S.P. Atre, Mudranika, Aurangabad, India: Shrimati T.V. Pathy, 1987.

Pennick, Nigel. *Geomancy: The Ancient Science of Man in Harmony with the Earth*. London: Thames and Hudson, 1979.

———. *Earth Harmony*. London: Century, 1987.

Penisten, John. *Hawaii: The Big Island, A Paradise Guide*. OR: Paradise Publications, 1989.

Peterson, Natasha. *Sacred Sites: A Traveler's Guide to North America's Most Powerful, Mystical Landmarks*. Chicago: Contemporary Books Inc., 1988.

Petsas, Photios. *Delphi: Monuments and Museum*. Athens, Greece: Krene Editions, 1981.

Pike, Donald G., and David Muench. *Anasazi: Ancient People of the Rock*. New York: Harmony Books, 1974.

Ponting, Margaret and Gerald. *New Light on the Stones of Callanish*. Callanish, Isle of Lewis: G. and M. Ponting, 1984.

Rachowiecki, Rob. *Peru: A Travel Survival Kit*. Berkeley, CA: Lonely Planet Publications, 1987.

Rafferty, Andrew, and Kevin Crossley Holland. *The Stones Remain: Megalithic Sites of Great Britain*. London: Rider, 1989.

Rai, Raghu and Usha. *Taj Mahal*. London: Times Books Ltd., 1986.

Reed, A.W. [illus. Roger Hart]. *Maori Myth and Legend*. Christchurch, New Zealand: A.H. and A.W. Reed Ltd., 1983.

Reid, Bill, and Robert Bringhurst. *The Raven Steals the Light*. Vancouver: Douglas and McIntyre, 1984.

Rice, William Hyde. *Hawaiian Legends*. Honolulu: Bishop Museum Press, 1977.

Riegert, Ray. *Hidden Hawaii: The Adventurer's Guide*. 4th ed. rev. Berkeley, CA: Ulysses Press, 1987.

Roberts, Ainslie, illus., and text by Charles Mountford. *The Dawn of Time: Australian Aboriginal Myths*. Blackwood, Australia: Art Australia, 1989.

———. *The First Sunrise: Australian Aboriginal Myths*. Blackwood, Australia: Art Australia, 1989.

Roberts, Ainslie and Melva Jean. *Dreamtime Heritage*. Blackwood, Australia: Art Australia, 1975.

Roberts, Anthony, ed. *Glastonbury: Ancient Avalon, New Jerusalem*. London: Rider and Co., 1978.

Roberts, David. *Sinai*. n.p.: Palphot Ltd., n.d.

Roberts, Melva Jean. *Echoes of the Dreamtime: Australian Myths in the Paintings of Ainslie Roberts*. Melbourne, Australia: J.M. Dent, 1980.

Rossner, Father John. *In Search of the Primordial Tradition and the Cosmic Christ*. St. Paul, MN: Llewellyn Publications, 1989.

Russell, Peter. *The Awakening Earth: Our Next Evolutionary Leap*. London: Routledge and Kegan Paul, 1982.

Sams, Jamie, and David Carson. *Medicine Cards: The Discovery of Power Through the Ways of Animals*. Sante Fe, NM: Bear and Co., 1988.

Schaafsma, Polly. *Indian Rock Art of the Southwest*. Albuquerque: University of New Mexico Press, 1980.

Schele, Linda, and Mary Ellen Miller. *Blood of Kings: Dynasty and Ritual in Mayan Art*. New York: George Braziller Inc. with Kimball Art Museum in Fort Worth, TX, 1986.

Screeton, Paul. *Quicksilver Heritage: The Mystic Leys—Their Legacy of Ancient Wisdom*. London: Sphere Books, 1977.

Seiden, Allan. *Flowers of Hawaii*. Honolulu: Island Heritage, 1986.

Seike, Kiyoshi. *Japanese Touch for Your Garden*. Tokyo: Kodansha International, 1980.

Service, Alastair, and Jean Bradbery. *A Guide to the Megaliths of Europe*. London: Granada, 1981.

Shearer, Tony. *Beneath the Moon and Under the Sun: A Re-appraisal of the Sacred Calendar and the Prophecies of Ancient Mexico*. Sante Fe, NM: Sun Books, 1975.

Shirakawa, Yoshikazu. *Himalayas*. New York: Abradale Press, Harry N. Abrams Inc., 1971.

Showker, Kay. *Jordan and the Holy Land*. New York: Fodor's Travel Guides, 1984.

Siers, James. *The Maori People of New Zealand*. Wellington: Sevenseas Publishing Pty. Ltd., 1980.

Silverberg, Robert. *The Mound Builders*. Athens, Ohio: Ohio University Press, 1989.

Simply Living magazine. vol. 4, #1, 1989.

Sinai Monuments: Monastery of St. Catherine. Cairo: Egyptian Antiquities Organization Press, 1986.

Smith, Peter. *The Baha'i Religion*. Oxford: George Ronald, 1988.

Sproul, Barbara C. *Primal Myths: Creating the World*. New York: Harper and Row, 1979.

Steiner, Rudolf. *Ancient Myths: Their Meaning and Connection with Evolution*. Vancouver: Steiner Book Centre Inc., 1971.

Sterling, Thomas. *The Amazon*. Amsterdam: Time Life, 1973.

Stewart-Smith, Jo. *In the Shadow of Fujisan*. London: Rainbird Publishing Group, 1987.

Stierlin, Henri. *The Cultural History of Pre-Columbian America*. London: Aurum Press Ltd., 1984.

Stone, Margaret. *Supernatural Hawaii*. Honolulu: Aloha Graphics and Sales, 1979.

Stuart, Gene S. *America's Ancient Cities*. Washington, DC: National Geographic Society, 1988.

Summerfield, John. *Fodor's 89 guide to the People's Republic of China*. New York: Fodor Travel Publications, 1988.

Sutphen, Dick. *Sedona: Psychic Energy Vortexes*. Malibu, CA: Valley of the Sun Printing Co., 1986.

Swan, James A. *Sacred Places: How the Living Earth Seeks Our Friendship*. Sante Fe, NM: Bear and Co., 1990.

Tobias, Michael Charles, and Harold Drasdo. *The Mountain Spirit*. New York: Overlook Press, 1979.

Tompkins, Peter. *Mysteries of the Mexican Pyramids*. New York: Harper and Row, 1976.

Trupp, Fritz. *The Last Indians: South America's Cultural Heritage*. Austria: Perlinger Verlag GmbH., 1981.

Van Kirk, Jacques and Parney. *Guide to Maya Sites of the Yucatan*. St. Petersburg, FL: Great Outdoors Publishing Co., 1987.

Verma, Umendra. *Aurangabad, Daultabad, Ellora and Ajanta*. New Delhi, India: Jayna Publishing, n.d.

Viele, Catherine W. *Voices in the Canyon*. Southwest Parks and Monuments Association, 1990.

Walsh, Grahame L. *Australia's Greatest Rock Art*. Bathurst, Australia: E.J. Brill/Robert Brown and Associates, 1988.

Waters, Frank. *Masked Gods*. New York: Ballantine Books, 1950.

Weiner, Jonathon. *Planet Earth: The Companion Volume to the PBS TV Series*. Bantam, 1986.

West, John Anthony. *Traveller's Key to Ancient Egypt*. London: Harrap Columbus, 1987.

Westwood, Jennifer, ed. *The Atlas of Mysterious Places*. New York: Weidenfeld and Nicolson, 1987.

White, Alan, and Bruce Epler. *Galapagos Guide*. Quito: Libri Mundi Libreria Int., 1982.

Wickert, Jürgen D. *Borobudur*. Jakarta, Indonesia: PT Intermasa, 1988.

Wild New Zealand. Sydney, Australia: The Reader's Digest, 1981.

Wilkens, W.J. *Hindu Mythology*. Delhi: Indological Book House, 1988.

Williamson, Ray. *Living the Sky: The Cosmos of the American Indian*. University of Oklahoma Press, 1984.

Wosien, Maria Gabriele. *Sacred Dance: Encounter with the Gods*. Avon, 1974.

Zambucka, Kristin. *The Keepers of the Earth*. Honolulu: Harrane Publishing Co., 1985.

Index